When it comes to great parenting, Ramsey and Cruze have hit the nail on the head with *Smart Money Smart Kids*. Every good parent should teach his child how to manage money and live responsibly, but until now, there was no manual. This is a top priority read for every parent.

— MEG MEEKER, M.D., author of the national bestseller, *Strong Fathers Strong Daughters*

This valuable guide, from two different perspectives—that of the parent and that of the child—is a great resource for families. It's chock-full of easy, practical, and smart ideas on how to raise productive, happy, and money-savvy kids. We'll definitely take it to heart!

— BRAD PAISLEY AND KIMBERLY WILLIAMS-PAISLEY, Grammy Award-winning artist / actress, director, and producer

One of the bedrock foundations of the Robertson family is passing on values to your children and teaching them how to expand a great legacy. There is not a better family than the Ramseys to teach the importance of passing on the value of handling money and the wisdom of building the right financial legacy. Dave and Rachel show how powerful a family can be when they work together, teach responsibility, and share with others what works and what doesn't. This book is Miss Kay approved!

— MISS KAY ROBERTSON, matriarch of the Robertson family from A&E's *Duck Dynasty*

Thank you, Dave and Rachel, for this rock-solid game plan to teach our kids the value of working, spending, saving, and giving as they grow into adults with financial confidence and integrity.

— ELISABETH HASSELBECK, co-host of *Fox & Friends* and best-selling author

Finally someone's written the perfect book to help me prepare my children for a strong financial future. In their book, *Smart Money Smart Kids*, Dave Ramey and his daughter Rachel Cruze masterfully equip parents to train their children. As a father to six kids, I strongly urge every parent to read this book, apply these principles, and change their family's legacy.

— CRAIG GROESCHEL, pastor of
LifeChurch and author of the *New York
Times* best-selling book, *Fight*.

Contained in the pages of this book is the information you and I have been waiting for all our lives. In *Smart Money Smart Kids*, the father-daughter team of Dave Ramsey and Rachel Cruze moves miles beyond financial theory or interesting ideas. Instead, they provide proof of principles about money that, when harnessed, produce the power to change our families for generations to come. Drop everything. Read this one now.

— ANDY ANDREWS, *New York Times*
best-selling author of *The Traveler's Gift*
and *The Noticer*

I can't imagine a more practical book on a more needed topic. Nor can I imagine a better team to write it. Thanks, Dave and Rachel. We will put your work to good use!

— MAX LUCADO, best-selling author
of *You'll Get Through This*

Practical, relevant, and encouraging. My only wish is that I had this twenty years ago when we were raising our three sons!

— STASI AND JOHN ELDREDGE, *New York
Times* best-selling authors of *Captivating*
and *Wild at Heart*

For years, our friend Dave Ramsey has taught us, inspired us, and at times threatened us to get our financial house in order. As if that wasn't enough, now he wants to brainwash our kids as well! And I'm so glad he does. In *Smart Money Smart Kids*, Dave and his extraordinary daughter Rachel Cruze team up to help us begin creating healthy financial family traditions. You're going to laugh, cry, and then come up with a plan to raise money-smart kids—a plan that will allow the generation coming along behind you to be ahead of you in one of the most critical arenas of life.

— ANDY STANLEY, senior pastor,
North Point Ministries

Dave Ramsey has created a financial system and tools that, if followed, will SAVE our economy. His daughter Rachel has been tutored in that gospel since birth. This book should be required reading for every parent that doesn't want to spend their retirement asking their 20-something-year-old child when they are going to move out and get a job!

— SHAY CARL, YouTube personality
and co-founder of Maker Studios

Dave Ramsey has more practical insight into money management than anybody on the planet.

— PASTOR RICK WARREN, founding pastor,
Saddleback Church, P.E.A.C.E. Plan

It's no surprise that Dave Ramsey and his daughter, Rachel, have put together a powerful book with practical ideas. With seven children in the Miller home, we're implementing *Smart Money Smart Kids* tactics and strategies and getting outstanding results!

— JOHN G. MILLER, author of *QBQ! The Question Behind the Question, Outstanding!*, and *Parenting the QBQ Way*

We have had the pleasure of knowing Dave Ramsey and his daughter Rachel Cruze since we moved to Nashville. You should know that after hearing Dave on the radio all these years that they actually live their lives the way he inspires us to live ours. Now Rachel joins her dad in the family business and writes this book that will help our children better understand money and how to build their lives with a richer understanding of financial responsibility. They talk the talk and walk the walk. Let's share this book with our kids and inspire them to run for Congress.

— TRACIE AND SCOTT HAMILTON

If you want to impart skills to your children in spending, saving, and giving, look no further than *Smart Money Smart Kids*! Dave and Rachel brilliantly present their plan with stories and hard-earned wisdom that will keep you flipping the pages for more. This book is a must-read for every parent wanting to extend grace while instilling the unchanging axioms of money management.

— EMERSON EGGERICHS, PH.D.,
author of *Love and Respect in the Family*

Smart Money Smart Kids

Raising the Next Generation to Win with Money

"Train up a child . . ."

PROVERBS 22:6

Smart Money Smart Kids

Raising the Next Generation to Win with Money

Dave Ramsey
Rachel Cruze

LAMPO PRESS
THE LAMPO GROUP, INC.

Published by Lampo Press, The Lampo Group, Inc.
Brentwood, Tennessee 37027

This publication is designed to provide accurate and authoritative information with
regard to the subject matter covered. It is sold with the understanding that the
publisher is not engaged in rendering financial, accounting or other professional
advice. If financial advice or other expert assistance is required, the services of a
competent professional should be sought.

Scripture quotations marked "NKJV" are taken from the New King James
Version®. Copyright © 1982 by Thomas Nelson, Inc. Used by permission. All
rights reserved.

Scripture quotations marked "NIV" are taken from the Holy Bible, New International
Version®, NIV®. Copyright © 1973, 1978, 1984, 2011 by Biblica, Inc.™ Used by
permission of Zondervan. All rights reserved worldwide.

Editors: Ken Abraham, Allen Harris, Jennifer Gingerich, Darcie Clemen
Cover design: Melissa McKenney
Interior design: Mandi Cofer
Cover photo credit: Parker Young

Library of Congress Cataloging-in-Publication Data

Ramsey, Dave.
  Smart money smart kids : raising the next generation to win with money
/ Dave Ramsey, Rachel Cruze.
    pages cm
  ISBN 978-1-9370-7763-1 (hardback)
  1. Children—Finance, Personal. 2. Finance, Personal. I. Cruze,
Rachel. II. Title.
  HG179.R31562 2014
  332.0240083—dc23

                        2014001650

Printed in the United States of America
14 15 16 17 18 BVG 5 4 3 2 1

Dedication

From Dave:

To the Ramsey kids, Denise, Rachel, and Daniel. You were the proving ground for everything written in this book. You showed us what worked—and what didn't. You guys *are* the change in our family tree.

To our first grandchild, William, and all your future brothers, sisters, and cousins. You are our legacy.

From Rachel:

To Mom and Dad, who not only taught me how to handle money, but also how to live a full life through hard work, perseverance, integrity, and a relationship with Jesus. Thank you for the example you've been to the Ramsey kids.

To Winston, my husband, my encourager, and my support. Thank you for cheering me on every step of the way. I am honored to be your wife and excited to pass this legacy down through our own family.

Acknowledgments

This book is more than twenty years in the making, and there's no way to capture every family member, friend, and team member who contributed to this endeavor in some way. So to all those whose names are too many to mention, thank you for helping us change our family tree and, in the process, launch a crusade to change an entire generation.

Special thanks to those who were hands-on in making this book possible:

Sharon Ramsey, Proverbs 31 wife and mother whose children rise up and call her blessed.

Winston Cruze, for your endless encouragement and support throughout this project.

Allen Harris and Jen Gingerich, a huge help with the writing and refining process.

Ken Abraham, a brilliant book editor and great friend.

Preston Cannon, for coordinating this entire project.

ACKNOWLEDGMENTS

Darcie Clemen, Ashley Edmonds, and Brandon Brison, for providing outstanding editorial, research, and project management support.

Brian Williams, Luke LeFevre, and Melissa McKenney, our creative geniuses responsible for overseeing all design elements and cover art.

Jen Sievertsen and Beth Tallent, the best marketing and publicity minds in the business.

Suzanne Simms, Jeremy Breland, Joel Rakes, Meg Grunke, Neal Webb, and too many others to mention for their time, leadership, prayers, and hard work throughout this process.

Contents

CONTENTS

Introduction

Dave: The first group I ever spoke to about how to handle money was a Rotary Club with forty-three people in the audience. I used an overhead projector, and I actually had hair. That was a long time ago, many air miles ago, and several million people in audiences ago. When I finished my big presentation that I had practiced for hours in front of the mirror, I walked to a table in the back of the room to sell copies of my little self-published book, *Financial Peace*, for twelve dollars each.

After I covered the basics of money (which is what I still do), everyone at the seminar agreed that common sense is not really all that common. I'm sure as that first person—a middle-aged woman—walked up to the book table, she saw a young speaker relieved that his big speech was finished. I will never forget her comment. Holding my little book, she looked at me and said, "Dave, that was great information. Why don't parents teach their children about money? Why don't we teach basic money skills like this in schools? Our kids need to know this information."

She was right. This mom knew she had never been taught how money works, and she felt inept. She knew she could learn and work toward a better understanding of money, but she also had a sense of sadness knowing that she had not taught her children about money. Nor had anyone else.

For the last several decades as I have done media, spoken to millions in audiences, and traveled America, that scene and those questions have been repeated thousands of times—"Why don't we teach our children common-sense money principles?"

Virtually all of us teach our children about things in which we feel competent. I have a friend whose dad is an excellent mechanic. That guy spent hours talking cars, laying under them or leaning over them. The dad and son built engines, played with gears, and did brake repairs every weekend and most evenings. And when they weren't working on something mechanical together, they were talking about it. Is it any wonder that my friend is a serious gearhead? He loves anything with a motor, and he is great at it. It is a family tradition.

I have another friend whose father was a two-term governor of our state and was the youngest governor in our state's history. So my buddy was a little boy living in the Governor's Mansion. That family spent most of their energy, time, and dinner conversations on politics or public service. He literally cut his teeth on politics. Just by being present, he was taught by osmosis. Is it any wonder that he loves politics, became a U.S. congressman, ran for mayor, and served in multiple high-ranking public service offices? He loves anything having to do with public service. It is a family tradition.

I have another friend whose mother is a well-known author.

... You finish the story. I have another friend whose father was always starting businesses, making them successful, then selling them. ... You finish the story. I have another friend whose father loves aircraft, piloting, and aircraft history. ... You finish the story.

We all have a family tradition. Sometimes it is a sad legacy, one that you work not to repeat. Children are sponges—they are going to absorb whatever is around them, so we need to be intentional about what surrounds them. The good news is you can choose your family tradition for the next generation. It is a choice.

People with wealth—who also have a healthy understanding of wealth—don't obsess about money or worship money. They are, however, intentional about how it is handled, and they make sure their children know how to handle money. It is a family tradition.

When my wife, Sharon, and I went broke, lost everything, and filed for bankruptcy, we were two twenty-eight-year-olds with a toddler and a brand-new baby. I did stupid things with money, which wrecked that portion of my life. When I discovered common-sense, biblically based financial principles and applied them, our lives started turning around and we began to win with money. As we got to where we could breathe, the first thought we had was to make sure financial stupidity never happened to the Ramsey family again. The second thought was to safeguard the next generation. We declared not only that *we* would never be in that situation again, but also that we would permanently sear proper money principles into our children's beings so *they* would never be in the same situation. We declared that we would change our family tree.

So Sharon and I, that scared and scarred young couple, made the declaration that where money was concerned, we would start a new family tradition—a tradition of money knowledge, money character traits, and wealth. The good news is, it worked. Our lives and family tree have been changed because we have raised three money-smart kids.

This book is about you starting a new family tradition with money. Rachel and I are going to teach you practical, tactical, spiritual, and strategic principles that will change your family tree. You will either intentionally teach your children how to handle money or they will live in your basement until they are forty. You will either model how to handle money or they will struggle like the rest of our culture, where common sense isn't common.

I will never tell you that the Ramseys have it all together or that we've done the things in this book perfectly every time. There were times I was an awful money dad. There were times Sharon folded under the pressure of a whining kid in a store aisle. We are not perfect, nor were we perfect when raising our money-smart kids. But we did model good money principles, and we tried hard to intentionally create teachable moments about money for our children.

You may be late to the party with older kids. You may be excellent with money or not. You may be just starting your family. Wherever you are, you can teach from today forward and begin a new family tradition with money. You don't have to be perfect, nor do you have to be paralyzed by the mistakes of the past. You simply have to start. You can start today and grow money-smart kids.

While we have never perfectly executed the money-smart principles we teach in this book, we have succeeded in raising money-smart kids. Of all the successes, accolades, and fame I have been blessed with, what I am most proud of are my children. Sharon and I have three competent, confident, poised, and wonderful adult children. They are winning at their spiritual walks, their marriages, and their careers, and all of them handle money well.

Our daughter Rachel has become a world-class communicator

teaching these principles to audiences of every age and size all across this country. Her favorite thing to do is guide and teach families how to start new money traditions like we did. Of course I am her proud dad, but as you read her words, you will quickly say to yourself, *I want to raise kids like her.* And you can.

The bottom line is this: If the Ramseys can go from stupidity on steroids, to bankruptcy, to a new family legacy and a new family money tradition, you can too. Hold on. This is going to be a wild and exciting ride.

CHAPTER ONE

I Was That Little Girl . . .

Rachel: "And we're back. Joining us now is Rachel Ramsey . . . er, I mean Rachel *Cruze*, the daughter of financial expert Dave Ramsey. Sorry about that, Rachel."

So goes the opening line of pretty much every television segment I've been on for the past several years—at least since I got married. I guess that's the danger in growing up Ramsey. My dad has developed such a huge reputation as "that money guy" for more than twenty years that a lot of the crowds I speak to or TV hosts I visit with just can't shake the association. And you know what? I'm totally fine with that. I'm proud of my family and the way I was brought up, but I always need to clarify something with those who only see the "Ramsey" instead of the "Rachel": My story is not like my parents' story.

I've never gone broke. I've never lost everything and declared bankruptcy. I've never felt the shame and pain of having bill collectors call at all hours of the day and night. I've never bought food and freaked out in the checkout line because I wasn't sure I'd have enough money afterward to pay the power bill. But my parents went through all of that and more.

I was six months old when Mom and Dad filed bankruptcy. Dad had been doing real estate deals for a few years at that point, and he had gotten pretty good at it. By the time he was twenty-six, he had a portfolio worth about $4 million. He and Mom had lived the high life for a while, and my older sister, Denise, was born at the peak of their success. Then, as a result of a lot of bad business decisions, just as Mom and Dad were trying to figure out how to be parents for the first time, everything fell apart.

Dad's whole business at the time was built on debt. He owed millions of dollars on his investments, and one day, the banks called his loans out of the blue. Problem was, he didn't have a few million bucks in the bank to pay the notes. He got sued. A lot. He describes it as "a bazillion times."

I was born in April 1988. Mom and Dad declared bankruptcy that September. Dad describes it like this: "After years of fighting it, with a toddler, a new baby, and a marriage hanging on by a thread, we hit bottom."

They hit hard.

But hey, I was only six months old. I had no concept of money. I didn't know how it felt to be broke or what it meant to be wealthy. I had never been on the fancy vacations or owned the expensive clothes and jewelry. Some might say I was born right at the worst time: the crash. I see it differently. I think I was born at the perfect time: the fresh start. I didn't have to see them *lose* everything; I got to see them *rebuild* everything and learn the lessons that have since helped countless other families get out of debt. That's the really exciting part!

Back in those days, Dad was doing a lot more than simply trying to figure out how to keep the lights on and food on the table. He was trying to figure out how money really works. And as a new Christian, he was trying to learn what the Bible says about money. Along the way, he started laying out some principles about how to handle money that eventually grew into a small Sunday School class, then a book, and then a full thirteen-week class that millions of families have now attended. He started hosting a daily talk radio show, which now has millions of listeners every week, and he wrote a handful of other books that walk families along the road to financial peace. Dad's definitely been busy!

It cracks me up when I hear people talk about "Dave Ramsey" like he is Bono or Mother Teresa. To me, he's just my dad. And all these books and tools and principles that people have used to take control of their money? All of that started in our living room.

You see, mine was the very first family to go through "the Dave Ramsey plan"—and trust me, it wasn't always easy. There's been a lot of fun that's come from being a Ramsey, but my older sister, Denise, my brother, Daniel, and I had to work—and work hard—for the blessings we've received. Being Dave Ramsey's daughter didn't guarantee that I'd never struggle with money; knowing and applying Dave Ramsey's principles did. This stuff works for me just like it will work for you.

I've been living and breathing these principles my whole life. Before I could walk, Mom and Dad were already fighting their way out of bankruptcy and starting to implement the principles that would eventually help other families get out of debt and win with money. Now, with a lifetime of training, I'm a professional speaker, and I travel the country teaching people the principles that my dad taught me.

My husband, Winston, and I are like any other family on the Dave Ramsey plan—we work, give, save, and spend in a way that's already setting up a legacy for our own future kids and grandkids. We do a monthly budget, we plan for big expenses, and we never even *consider* debt a useful tool. From the very beginning, my parents gave me a legacy of debt-free living, and that's one of the best gifts any parent could ever give their kids.

It Happens Every Day

Every day, people call into *The Dave Ramsey Show* to scream at the top of their lungs, "WE'RE DEBT FREE!" These are families who have been working hard, sometimes for several years, to get out of debt and change their family tree forever. These are moms and dads who have been working two or three or five jobs to break the chains of debt. They've fought and climbed their way out from under a pile of car loans, credit card bills, and student loans, and they are excited. There's something in their voices when they tell their story; you know they will never again put their family back into debt.

Often, these families drive to our office to do their debt-free call from our lobby. We have this awesome café in our lobby called Martha's Place that always smells like cinnamon rolls and fresh-baked cookies. Think of it like walking into your grandmother's kitchen on Christmas morning, like you're stepping into a cloud of homemade joy. Trust me; it's amazing.

Martha's Place sits opposite of Dad's radio studio, so visitors and debt-free callers can come in and watch Dad do the show through a glass wall separating the studio from the lobby. Sometimes I'll see a family walk in, and I'll know immediately why they're here. I can tell they're a mix of exhausted and excited and usually a little nervous. It's easy to see that they've been in a car for several hours to get here. The dad stretches out his back while a shy little four-year-old girl wraps her arms around his leg. The mom walks in holding a sleeping baby. And then there's a hyper seven-year-old boy who hits the lobby like a horse coming out of the gates at the Kentucky Derby!

Martha greets them and helps round up the kids. She sets them up with the headset and microphone and stands them in the right spot where they can see Dave inside the studio. And then, it's time. After years of working overtime and extra jobs, after overcoming a lifetime of bad money decisions, after driving a stake in the ground and changing the course of their family legacy, it's time to tell their story on the radio.

As the mom and dad share the microphone, both jumping in to tell parts of the story, you can see the little boy and girl getting excited. They know they have a job to do—they've been practicing it in the car for the whole five-hour drive. They're waiting for the cue from their parents. Then you hear Dave say those magic words, "Okay guys, count it down."

And this mom and dad, who have moved mountains to change the direction of their family, bend down so the little boy and girl can reach the microphone. You'll hear the dad say, "Are you ready, guys? Just like we practiced. Three . . . two . . . one . . ." And then, together with mom and dad, you'll hear these precious little chipmunk voices yell as loud as they can, "WE'RE DEBT FREE!"

I cry almost every time. I just want to walk up to that little girl, put her face in my hands, look her in the eyes, and say, "Do you have any idea what your parents just did for you? They have changed your entire life."

You see, *I was that little girl*. After my parents' bankruptcy, they could have gone right back into the old habits that got them into trouble in the first place. But they didn't. They changed. They changed their own lives, and in the process, they changed the kind of life I could have. They taught me the keys I need to win with money for life.

Growing Up Ramsey

By the time I came along, Mom and Dad's days of spending money hand over fist were gone for good. Shopping with Mom always meant at least five minutes in the checkout line sorting coupons. More than one of the stores we frequented nicknamed her "Coupon Lady." I don't think I've ever seen her pay full price for anything. She has a keen radar for clearance racks. She can whip out a coupon for just about anything. You think Dave Ramsey knows how to work a pair of scissors to cut up credit cards? You should see Sharon Ramsey go to town on the Sunday newspaper ads! Dad probably learned his famous scissor techniques from her!

I never realized that we lived differently than other families. It didn't occur to me that other moms walked into a store, pulled an expensive dress off the rack, and paid full price for it. That probably would have felt weird to me because I certainly never saw my mom do that! And wasn't every family's favorite vacation destination a public campground? No? Huh. Just us, I guess.

The tight financial situation sometimes bugged me on Sunday afternoons. The Ramsey family went to church every Sunday. I sat in the pew in my sister's hand-me-down dresses, tights, and patent leather shoes, and when it was time for the offering, I dropped in my dollar bill that I had taken out of my "Give" envelope (I'll talk about this later). Giving was always a priority for our family. No matter how tight things got, Mom and Dad always modeled faithful, consistent giving, and they made sure we kids participated too. That was huge for us.

Anyway, after church all of our friends would pile into their cars and head to local restaurants. Denise and I would begin begging to go out to eat before we even reached the car. And every week, Dad said something like, "We're going to the best restaurant in town! *The best!* Nobody is going to eat better than we are today!"

Early on, Denise and I would fall for it. The more he built it up, the more excited we got. We'd jump up and down and start asking, "Where are we going? Where are we going?"

With a lot of drama, Dad would exclaim, "We're going to Sharon's Kitchen!" Translation: Once again, the Ramseys were eating Sunday lunch at home. Good thing our mom's a great cook!

I laugh about those times, but the truth is, they shaped me into who I am today. I know it wasn't easy for Mom and Dad to stay focused for so long. I'm sure they would have loved to have eaten out every week with their friends from church too. But they had to tell themselves what they often told us: "It's not in the budget." And so we pulled up our chairs at Sharon's Kitchen and somehow made it the best restaurant in town. Even after all these years, it's still one of my favorites.

Joining the Revolution

By the time I entered kindergarten, our financial situation started to stabilize. We weren't totally out of the woods yet, but the worst of the crisis was behind us. Dad had learned a lot about how to handle money, and around that time, he started putting it together in a class that would become *Financial Peace University* (FPU). At first, he offered it one night a week at a local Holiday Inn. The community's interest in FPU started slowly, but it soon began to pick up steam. When the Monday night class filled up, he started a new class on another night. And then another. Before long, Dad was teaching FPU classes five nights a week. Now, more than twenty years later, millions of families have changed their lives by going through the class!

Clearly, common-sense financial education struck a nerve, first in our community and then around the country. What my dad was teaching grew into something more than a class, seminar, book, or radio show. It became a *revolution*.

Now I'm part of that revolution. I'm on a crusade to help families avoid huge financial disasters altogether. I help parents put their kids on solid financial ground from day one. I talk to teenagers and college students and show them how to be money-smart and live debt free before they ever have the chance to go into debt. That's what my parents did for me, and that's what I want to share with young families and students.

I like to say that my dad is the emergency surgeon, and I'm the preventative medicine. Nobody gets people out of a financial crisis like Dave Ramsey, but we'd both prefer it if people never got into that kind of mess in the first place. That's become my crusade.

In the following chapters, I'll walk you through what it means to raise money-smart kids. I'll explain how I learned the importance of a strong work ethic, and we'll explore specific ways you can pass that on to your children. I'll teach you what my parents taught me about spending, saving, and giving. We'll talk about debt, why it's so devastating for young people, and how to teach your kids to avoid it—especially when it's time to head to college or buy a car. We'll tackle some tougher topics like entitlement, enabling, and contentment so that you can help your kids define what "enough" means for them. We'll talk about relationships and how money often gets in the way, sometimes actually destroying families and friendships. And finally, we'll talk about how to raise children who have the emotional, spiritual, and moral backbones to receive the financial legacy you might leave them one day.

I am so proud of my parents and how hard they worked to turn our family around all those years ago. They faced and overcame things I can't imagine, but in the process, they put me in a position to win in a way *they* probably couldn't have imagined themselves. I have never owed a dime to anyone. I *will never* owe a dime to anyone. I have been raised in genuine, lasting financial peace. That's not because I'm "Dave Ramsey's daughter." It's because my parents took the time and made the extra effort to teach me how to handle money. Because of them, I have complete confidence in my ability to manage my finances, no matter how much or how little I have. That is the best feeling in the world, and it's an incredible gift you can give your kids too!

Right now, you may be fighting some of the same battles my parents fought all those years ago. Or maybe you've already won those struggles and you want to help your kids avoid them completely. Either way, you're in the right place. No matter where you are financially right now, whether you're struggling or winning with money, I can give you a perspective you desperately need: the perspective of your children. After all, all those years ago, I *was* that little girl.

CHAPTER TWO

Work

It's NOT a Four-Letter Word

Rachel: When I was in fifth grade, I spent an afternoon at a friend's house and saw the weirdest thing. I watched my friend's mom clean her room, take our dishes to the sink after we ate, put her laundry away, feed the dog, and take out the trash, never once stopping to ask us to help. Right then, I knew my family was different.

I've learned so much from my parents over the years, but one of the most fundamental lessons they taught me from a young age was that the Ramseys are hard workers. People may know about Dad's radio show, our *Financial Peace University* class, our high school curriculum, our youth Bible study materials, or any of the dozens of other products and services we offer, but if you're wondering what the Ramsey "family business" is, let me tell you from experience—the family business is *work*.

As an adult, I look back at my childhood and I'm extremely

thankful for all my parents did for me. But there's one thing they taught me that I lean on literally every day of my life, and that's how to work. I learned early on that work creates discipline, and when you have discipline in your life, you are a healthier person.

There is no better feeling than coming home from a job and feeling tired. You know, the *good kind* of tired. The kind of tired that means you actually *did* something with your life today. Instead of allowing the next generation to sit in front of the computer or PlayStation all day, being lazy and lethargic, let your kids experience the feeling of being tired after some good, old-fashioned work. Raking leaves, cleaning the house, or being responsible for feeding the pet creates a sense of accomplishment, the sense that they actually did something that they can feel good about. It makes them feel confident that they can go out and win.

Dave: Our culture has made many wonderful advances to ensure the safety and well-being of children. But we may have taken this too far. Many parents today are so centered on what their children want that they have lost perspective on what their children really *need*. Perspective—looking at life over time—demands that you teach children to work. Teaching children to work is not child abuse. We teach them to work not for our benefit, but because it gives them both dignity in a job well done *today* and the tools and character to win *in the future* as adults.

You should view teaching your children to work in the same way you view teaching them to bathe and brush their teeth—as a necessary skill for life. An adult who has no clue how to tackle a job and finish it with vigor is as debilitated as an adult with green teeth and body odor. If your child graduates from high school and his only skill set consists of playing video games, whining, copping an attitude of entitlement, and eating junk food, you have set him up to fail.

Another huge benefit of teaching a child the wonder of work is that she will tend to lose respect for people who refuse to work. Why is this good? It is good because you want your daughter to marry Mr. Right, not Mr. Lazy. We noticed quickly that our daughters (and our son) didn't pursue relationships with people who didn't know how to work. This is great news, because someday you may have grandkids, and you want both of their parents to be productive so your grandkids get to eat.

Rachel: Cleaning our rooms was a standard chore in our house—one that I hated! I am not a super-organized person in general, and this trait was definitely worse when I was younger. Week after week, I was told to clean my room, and I put it off as long as I could . . . at least until I heard footsteps coming up the stairs to examine my work. Mom and Dad didn't expect our rooms to look like military barracks, but they did expect them to look neat and nice. And even though I didn't particularly enjoy the process, after spending just a few minutes cleaning and seeing the results, it was rewarding. I immediately saw what my hard work had accomplished, and it felt great.

Work might be a challenge for your children, especially if they aren't used to it, but what a blessing to give your kids. Of course, I'm talking about age-appropriate work; nevertheless, the value of work is needed and necessary. Proverbs 22:6 says, "Train up a child in the way he should go, and when he is old he will not depart from it" (NKJV). When your kids learn hard work from a young age, the habit will stick with them for life.

Now, my dad is one of those people who never seems to have

much trouble figuring out how to make money. Sure, Mom and Dad had some trouble *keeping* it for a little while during the bankruptcy years, but bringing home a good income was never really a problem. That's because my parents have never been confused about where money comes from. It's something my dad has told me pretty much every day of my life: Money comes from work.

Even when my parents went bankrupt, it wasn't because Dad didn't work hard enough. He worked like crazy all the way up the ladder of success and down to their financial crash. Before the bankruptcy, Dad worked to build his fortune; after the bankruptcy, he worked to keep food on the table. The motivation changed, but the work ethic never did. My dad's the hardest working person I've ever seen.

He used to tell me stories about helping out with his parents' real estate business when he was a little boy. My grandparents worked out of their home, so when the phone rang, there was a good chance that it was a client. That meant when eight-year-old Dave answered the phone, he did it like a full-time, highly trained receptionist. And my mom grew up on a farm, so she was no stranger to hard work either. She could probably out-work all of us all day every day and still get home in time to host an amazing dinner party!

Dave: As Rachel said, my parents were in the real estate business when I was growing up. That was "back in the day" when phones had cords and rotary dials. "Back in the day" when people still read newspapers and bought houses from things called classified ads in newspapers and real estate magazines. "Back in the day" when there were no cell phones, voice mail, email, Twitter, Facebook, or even answering machines. So you had to answer the phone or it didn't get answered. When someone called my childhood home, they could be calling about buying a house, so if we didn't answer the telephone properly or if we handled the call incorrectly, the sale could be lost. Answering the phone well was a big deal.

We were taught early to greet the caller in a friendly and professional tone, especially when our parents were not available. We were taught to use our manners—"yes, sir" or "yes, ma'am" as opposed to "yeah"—and to take the caller's phone number and information and then repeat it back to them for verification. This respectful manner of handling the phone was a standard part of our lives, and there was no tolerance for mishandling it. We understood early on the concepts of customer service and entrepreneurism. I guess that is why Sharon and I drilled those same kinds of things into our kids—and why I still can't stand an unanswered phone.

MAKE NO ALLOWANCES

Rachel: Work was never an option in the Ramsey house, no matter how young Denise, Daniel, and I were. From the time I was five years old, I was working—*on commission*. Mom and Dad didn't believe in giving us an "allowance." Dad hated that word. It implies that a child is "allowed" a certain amount of money just for living and breathing. Sure, every parent likes to bless his or her child with surprises and gifts, but the allowance system as a general rule doesn't teach the child how real life works. My parents didn't want to raise kids who expected life to make "allowances" for them. We see that way too much in today's world.

There's a whole generation growing up thinking money is free. They expect their parents to keep paying their bills into adulthood, or they think the government exists to care for them. That mindset has never been an option for me—not even when I was a little kid!

From age five on, I operated on one general rule about making money: *Work, get paid; don't work, don't get paid.* That's a basic principle that a lot of parents miss with their little kids. If a child can understand that money comes from work at age four, then she'll be ready to hit the "real world" running at age twenty-four.

Dave: I do hate the word *allowance* because I think words are powerful and can convey deeper meanings. When you make *allowance* for someone, it is because they are not *able.* Allowances for children sound like welfare to me, as if children are unwilling or unable to achieve, so we have to cover for them. Granted, they are our children and we do cover for them, but Sharon and I wanted to instill drive and dignity in our kids' characters. These qualities do not develop when we hand everything to our kids, because then we give them the impression that they are the center of the universe. Handing out money and not teaching strong work habits create people who whine, who feel entitled, and who become perpetual victims. Does this sound like any adults you know? We taught our kids that the Bible says, "If anyone will not work, neither shall he eat" (2 Thessalonians 3:10), and we would quote verses like Proverbs 12:11: "He who tills his land will be satisfied with bread, but he who follows frivolity is devoid of understanding" (NKJV).

I once took a radio call from a father of a rebellious fourteen-year-old son. The father said his son refused to do chores and help around the house. So this dad went to his workshop, got a hammer, and placed it on the teen's plate at the dinner table. When his son came to dinner, the dad said, "No food until your chores are done, and if you continue to avoid your work, I am going take that hammer and break your plate." We all know that the fastest way to a teenage boy's heart is through his stomach. Not surprisingly, that young man immediately got to work. That may have been a drastic way to get the boy's attention, but I guarantee he will probably tell this story to his children and grandchildren because it got the point across and hopefully set a new pattern for his life.

Rachel: It is so important for parents to help their kids make the work-money connection from an early age. That means instead of an allowance, you should reframe the whole discussion with your kids. When speaking of money, "allowance" shouldn't even be in your children's vocabulary. Use the word "commission," and explain how money comes from work. As soon as your children understand cause-and-effect relationships, you can start teaching them the relationship between work and money.

The Fear Most Parents Have

Without fail, every time I'm on the road speaking to groups, I have a parent ask me, "How can I raise my kids not to feel entitled? How can I teach them the value of a dollar?" From my experience, the basic principle of working is one of the best ways to combat the attitude of entitlement. Once your kids understand that money comes from work, they won't be able to spend money on a toy without considering how much work went into actually *making* that money. Sure, they can and should enjoy a good purchase, but working for it makes every purchase—even a toy or video game—feel like an accomplishment, not an entitlement. Encourage your kids to discover the dignity of working and earning money themselves. The worst thing you can do is become a human ATM and give your kids a five, ten, or twenty-dollar bill every time they ask.

START THEM YOUNG: AGES THREE TO FIVE

I've talked to many parents who tried the commission system with their children as young as three or four years of age, and they've been shocked by how their kids have responded. Kids will jump on board with new things—yes, even money-type things—quicker than you may realize. You can create incredible teachable moments when you give your young children an opportunity to do a few things around the house and get paid for doing them.

Jobs for Little Kids

A word of caution: Some parents get so excited when teaching their kids about money that they go a bit . . . well, let's just say they go a bit overboard. Call me crazy, but telling your four-year-old to do the dishes every night and mow the lawn every weekend probably won't work out too well.

Remember, you're not opening up a sweatshop. For young children, I recommend that you limit the number of chores—somewhere around three jobs—and keep them short and simple. You want each job to be enough that it feels like a big accomplishment, but not so much that it seems complicated or impossible to complete. Some great options for chores at this age include:

- Picking up toys
- Putting dirty clothes in the laundry basket

- Making his or her own bed
- Matching socks in the clean laundry
- Setting the dinner table (with supervision)
- Collecting the indoor trash cans from around the house
- Helping carry in light groceries

The job assignments are up to you. Just list a handful of responsibilities your child is capable of doing and put a dollar amount on each one. You might be surprised at how excited your child gets about this. A friend of mine explained this system to his four-year-old daughter for the first time one Saturday morning, and her playroom went from looking like a tornado blew through it to "spick and span" in under thirty minutes. Not a bad return for a dollar!

Pay Fast and with Excitement!

When you're initiating the commission system with kids under age 5, you should pay them as soon as the job is complete. They need that immediate connection between the work they did and the money you're handing them. Younger kids don't relate the action and the reward if payment is delayed, especially by several days.

Let's be honest. When a four-year-old cleans his room, we all know that probably means Mom or Dad put away ten toys and the child put away two or three. That's okay. The goal at this age is to get the child in a mindset of working. That's not going to happen overnight. As long as your kids understand what the job is and what it means to see it through to the end, you're doing just fine.

As soon as your children finish the job, you should inspect

the work. You've got to really amp up the enthusiasm here. Get excited! If they cleaned their room, then they need to feel like they are the most incredible room-cleaners on the face of the earth! It may sound silly, but you're doing two things by expressing your excitement: You're showing them how proud *you* are of the work they've done, and you're building up *their own* pride in their hard work. At that point, handing them their commission for the job doesn't come across as an expectation; it comes across for what it is: payment for a job well done. That's the kind of mindset you want to encourage.

Make It Visual

Another key for rewarding kids between the ages of three and five is to make their commissions visual. With older children, you'll use the envelope system for setting money aside for saving, spending, and giving. But when you're just starting out with really young kids, it's a good idea to make the money look as big and impressive as possible. That means keeping it all together.

My dad taught me a great method for making fifty dollars look like $1 million to a five-year-old. Use a clear container and pay in dollar bills instead of loose change. As you put the bills in the container, be sure to rustle them up just a little bit. A stack of dollar bills can look pretty thin if it's lying flat, but if you get the bills wrinkled and a little wadded up, they start to look a lot bigger and more impressive when you see them in a clear container. Kids are visual learners, so it's great visual reinforcement to watch the money grow.

You want your children to imagine the bills exploding out of that jar. That kind of stuff gets them excited about their money, and they *should* be excited about it—after all, they earned it!

The Main Goal: Spend

When you have a three-, four-, or five-year-old, getting them to do a few chores and paying them is an incredible head start. Most children this age can't fully grasp money concepts like setting some aside for saving and spending (we will get there soon; don't worry). So the best way to reward young children is to go shopping with some of the money they have earned. Can you imagine how proud they will feel when they hand the cashier a couple of dollar bills that they earned all by themselves? Something amazing happens in little boys and girls when they get to walk into a store, pick out a toy all by themselves, and pay for it with money they earned.

GROW THEM UP: AGES SIX TO THIRTEEN

As your children grow, the chores, responsibilities, and maybe even the dollar amounts should grow to reflect their ability and maturity. As I got older, I wanted to do more things and buy more stuff, just like any other kid. We knew Mom and Dad would always take care of our necessities such as food and clothing, but Denise, Daniel, and I were under no illusion that our parents were there to fund every little thing we wanted to do. That meant as our wants and needs grew, so did our chores.

Make a List, Check It Twice

We continued to get paid commissions on the work we did around the house as we got older. I remember having a list of five specific chores, and I got paid one dollar for each of those five jobs. This wasn't back-breaking labor; I'm talking about tasks such as making my bed, taking out the trash, feeding the dog, jobs like that.

We had a chore chart on the fridge to keep track of who did what and how much we earned. Mom wrote our names on the chart and listed each of our five jobs. When we completed each task, we were supposed to put a check mark next to the chore to show that we did it.

Now does that mean I got a dollar every time I put my dirty dishes in the sink? No way! There are always going to be things kids should do around the house just because they're a member of the family. For us Ramsey kids, most of those unpaid chores revolved around mealtimes. We didn't get paid for setting the table, taking our dishes to the sink, or drying the dishes. If you were part of the family, cleaning the kitchen was simply expected.

You want your kids to understand that money comes from work, but you don't want to go so far that they end up thinking they should get paid for *everything* they do around the house. Money can't be the motivator every time; we all have to do some jobs simply because they're part of life.

You, as the parent, should figure out a handful of specific chores and a dollar amount for each one. That's your call. As I said, my parents paid me a dollar for each of my five specific chores. That's just what worked for them. The types of chores and specific amounts that work for your family are up to you.

Dave: Every time Rachel or I present the commission idea to a group of parents, we have at least one parent who disagrees with us. They argue that children should do work around the house just because they are part of the family, and they should not expect to get paid. I agree, but if you don't involve a money transaction in a few chores, you lose all the teachable moments in the work, spend, save, and give principles. Our children had a few chores that were paid commission items, and the rest of the work they did because they were part of the family. It is an act of love to help your mom or dad with the dishes, and it is not an *optional* act of love. These non-paid chores help teach kids how to be good citizens of their church or community, later producing adults who willingly volunteer to help others.

I grew up in a wonderful *Leave It to Beaver* neighborhood. It was a new suburb in Nashville, and almost all the families were first generation off the farm. Farmers are hard workers, so physical work was a part of our neighborhood, as was pitching in to help with projects other neighbors had going. Of course, no one expected to get paid; we were just helping our neighbors.

Our next-door neighbor was one of the nicest men I have ever known. He was kind and gentle and would help anyone in need. He was also a mechanical genius and enjoyed fixing and building things. He built hotrods from the ground up in his garage. And he could weld and turn a wrench on just about anything. To accomplish his hobbies, he collected stuff in his backyard—I mean a lot of stuff. As an adult, I look back and wonder what conversations took place among the adults, but all I knew was that every so often, all the neighborhood kids and many of the adults would show up to help John clean up his backyard.

We worked for hours moving and piling scrap metal, filling trucks with things to be hauled to the dump, and mowing and trimming the yard. We kids thought it was great fun, and everyone loved John and enjoyed helping him. When the yard was finally clean, all the kids were allowed to jump in the back of John's pickup truck for a ride down to the Kwik Sak for an ICEE. Our pay for a half-day's work was an ICEE. Well, not really. The real pay was that forty-five years later, I look back on the lessons those mornings taught me:

hard work, working with others, and, of course, repaying the kindness of a helpful neighbor with a simple cleanup day. You may think this was just a bunch of rednecks who let their kids ride in the back of a pickup, and you might be right. But those neighborhood work days played a huge role in making me the man I am today.

Adventures in Babysitting

Rachel: By the time I turned twelve, I received weekly commissions for my home chores, but I remember wanting to do more. Some of my friends at that time were babysitting. Now if you can imagine, I don't do things halfheartedly. If I was going to take on this new venture of watching other people's kids, I was going to do it right.

As I planned out my new endeavor, I focused on presentation and customer service. When a family was interested in hiring me to watch their kids, I would meet them and walk them through my presentation binder that highlighted my skills, experience, references, and fee schedule. Later, if they scheduled me—and seriously, who *wouldn't* hire a professional babysitter like that—I had them complete a form I created that included the hours they planned to be away, where and how I could reach them, emergency phone numbers and contact people, and any special needs or instructions I'd need to know. You can just call me Little Dave if you'd like.

It didn't take much time to put my binder and forms together, but it made a huge difference in my business. Dad always taught me that doing little things like that made me stand out from the crowd, which made me more marketable. Even if I didn't know what "marketable" meant at age twelve, I could definitely tell that I was getting more babysitting jobs than my friends.

Jobs for Older Kids and Tweens

When your kids are in the six- to thirteen-year-old age range, you need to upgrade their chores. By six, they are ready for a little more responsibility, so you can start to add more jobs and provide less hands-on help as they complete them. We recommend listing their tasks on a chore chart and sticking it on the fridge so they see it every day. Make a big deal when they complete a task and check off the item as done. Some great household jobs for this age range include:

- Making their own beds
- Feeding pets
- Vacuuming and sweeping
- Sorting, folding, and putting away laundry
- Cleaning the dishes
- Watering plants
- Cleaning windows
- Washing the car
- Doing yard work
- Cleaning the bathroom

As they get a little older, you can encourage them to find some ways to make money outside your home. You can help them brainstorm new ideas, such as:

- Babysitting
- Walking dogs
- Doing yard work for others

If your child has an entrepreneurial spirit, encourage that by helping make fliers to advertise his or her new business.

Pay Weekly

At this age, you can start paying commissions weekly instead of immediately. By now, your children should have already learned the crucial work-money connection, so it isn't as important to have the immediate reward of a payout. Knowing that they have to work *throughout the week* but they'll only get paid *once a week* teaches kids lessons in delayed gratification and patience. Besides, that's how the real world works, right?

In our house, every Sunday night was "payday," so we would grab our chore charts off the refrigerator, see whether or not we had completed all of our jobs, and then Dad would pay us for the work. If I only did three of my five chores, then guess what? I got three dollars, not five. Our parents never paid us for work we didn't do. That's not how life works, and it's not how our family functioned either. When we first started doing this, it was text-book. Every Sunday night, Dad would have fifteen one-dollar bills in his hand, ready to pay commissions to three eager kids. But every so often, on a Sunday night we would ask about payday and Dad would say, "I forgot to go to the bank and get the one-dollar bills, so we'll make it up next week." This was rare, but it *did* happen—even to Dave Ramsey. So parents, give yourself some grace. The more consistent you are, obviously, the better it is for your kids, but don't stress over it if you miss one payday. This small error probably won't send them to counseling.

Dave: As I look back on parenting the Ramsey kids and teaching the ideas of commission, chore charts, saving, giving, and spending, what amazes me most is that our kids still got it despite how often Sharon and I messed up. We talked about the concepts and enforced the "no work, no pay" principle, but we were far from exact in all the applications. If one of our kids messed up or broke something, we dished out grace and paid anyway. We just wanted them to get the concepts. My memory of Sunday-night payday is that we probably missed or forgot 25 percent or more of those, and yet our kids remember being taught these concepts thoroughly.

There will be times when you'll be too tired, on vacation, or simply distracted and forget to do "payday," but you can always make it up the next week by talking through the chores and carefully funding each child's three envelopes. So parent to parent, let me tell you the word here is *grace*—grace for the kids' reactions to unusual circumstances and grace for yourself for not perfectly executing this plan. You don't check every homework paper (Please tell me you don't check every single paper! That's a little weird.), and yet your kids will graduate and possibly even get good grades. The reason for this is that the child gets the concept of hard work and will do his or her part once you teach and model the principle. The key is to be intentional and to control the teaching and guiding of their character rather than to control the child.

Envelope System for Kids

Rachel: This is also the perfect time to start teaching your children about what to do with the money they're making. We're going to suggest you have your children divide their income across three key areas: spending, saving, and giving.

Give each child three specific envelopes: one named *Spend*, one named *Save*, and one named *Give*. Write those words big and bold across the envelope or let the kids decorate their envelopes however they want. Every dollar they earn in commission needs to be spread across these envelopes. You can also apply this to any birthday or gift money they receive throughout the year.

Here's how it worked for us on Sunday nights: I would take the five dollars I earned and put one dollar in the Give envelope (because giving always came first in our family), two dollars in the Save envelope, and two dollars in the Spend envelope. That's the most basic form of budgeting, but it works—even for a six-year-old.

The Spend envelope was fair game. We could use that however we wanted. It was meant to be *enjoyed* because money can be fun!

The Save envelope was basically a long-term Spend envelope. I wasn't saving for college or a house or anything at that age. My parents encouraged us to set savings goals, like for a certain toy that would take weeks or months to earn enough money to buy. As our savings grew and we hit our goal, we'd proudly take the Save envelope to the store and bring home our major purchase. This teaches your little ones about patience, goal-setting, and delayed gratification—three things a lot of adults still struggle with!

The Give envelope was extremely important in our house, which is why it was the first thing we did with our money. By the time I was six, my parents had stopped giving me *their* money to drop in the offering plate at church, and I took *my own* money from my Give envelope. Giving his own money changes a child's whole understanding of giving. We'll talk more about that later on.

GET THEM OUT: AGES FOURTEEN TO COLLEGE

When each of us kids in the Ramsey family turned fourteen, we graduated out of the Sunday night "payday" and into a checking account. Mom and Dad took the amount of money they would normally spend on us for entertainment, clothes, and other needs, and they put that amount of cash into our personal checking accounts each month. If the Ramsey teens wanted to spend more money, we knew where that money had to come from, so we got to work. Denise and I babysat a lot, Daniel did a number of odd jobs, and all three of us worked in Dad's office during the summers. We were all busy with social events, school activities, and sports, but that didn't stop us from working.

Opening My Own Business

When I was about fourteen, Dad sat my sister and me down and told us we needed to open our own business. As you can imagine, Denise and I blankly stared back at him with our fourteen- and sixteen-year-old eyes, thinking he was crazy. I said, "Dad, that's nuts! Why in the world do we need to open our own business?" If you know anything about my dad, you can imagine him getting excited about the idea and going on and on about profit and loss statements, managing products, and learning how to be entrepreneurs.

When we realized that he was serious, we started brainstorming how we were going to pull off our own business. Then we thought of the perfect job. At the time, Dad's growing company was filled with more than 150 team members. Do you know what hardworking people really like at work? Food! I'm talking about chips, candy bars, nuts, cookies, and granola bars. And lots of soft drinks and bottled water to finish it off. Denise and I basically stumbled upon a goldmine!

Dad always told us, "If you fail to plan, you plan to fail." Translation: There was no chance that he would allow us to simply show up at the office and sell snacks out of a box. If this was going to be a business, we had to *run* it like a business. That meant before the owner (Dad) allowed us into his building, we had to write up a full business plan. Yes, I'm serious. That plan detailed where we would purchase the snacks and how we would pay for our start-up inventory (which Dad graciously donated to us), price our products, manage our stock, run our profit and loss statement every week, and even evaluate our competition. That's right: competition! There were vending machines on each floor of the building, so we had to set our prices lower to attract customers.

Denise had a car by then, so every week the two of us went to the local discount warehouse and fought our way through the crowded aisles pushing a flatbed cart stacked with candy bars, chips, cookies, and cases of canned drinks. I remember barely being able to push that giant cart because it weighed more than Denise and me combined! Once we finally got all of our inventory into the car, we'd drive it over to the office, borrow a hand truck from shipping, and unload the car ourselves. Then we'd make our rounds through all the different break rooms around the building, setting up and restocking our display racks. By now you may think I am joking, but this is as true as it comes.

We replenished the snacks and soft drinks weekly, but Denise and I were both in school all day during the week, so there was no one left to "mind the store." That meant we had to rely on the honor system. We posted our prices next to the displays and set out a collection jar for the money. There was only one rule for Dad's team members: Don't eat it if you can't pay for it! That worked great . . . until the money came up short a couple of weeks in a row. I thought Dad was going to lose his mind. His own team members were ripping off his daughters! It's kind of funny when we look back on it.

That led to a quick rebranding of our little enterprise. From that day on, our business was known as "Your Integrity Snacks." If someone was going to take something without paying, then they had to steal from a business called "Your Integrity"!

For a few years, it seemed like Denise and I made a small fortune in loose change. I remember the first big purchase we made for the business was an automatic change sorter and money roller. We saved up for it and instead of manually putting each coin into a coin wrapper, we had this marvelous machine to do it for us. It was the best and only investment we made in Your Integrity Snacks. But every week we took stacks of rolled coins to the bank. And, of course, we had to keep our profit and loss statement updated, showing our gross income minus our expenses, which left us with a pretty nice profit every week—even after Denise charged me gas money.

The snack shop idea was so simple, but it actually made some pretty good money for us. More than the money, though, it taught two young teenagers how to run a business, serve customers, and turn a profit. Looking back, I'm pretty sure that's really why Dad suggested we do it.

Jobs for Teens

By the time I was a teenager, I really understood the work-money connection. And one thing I didn't do was nickel and dime my parents to death. They took care of my necessities and a lot of fun stuff, too; however, I never assumed they'd just give me money for whatever I wanted to do. Parents, please understand when I say we weren't little chore-working soldiers marching around the house. Mom and Dad maintained a great balance with us when it came to work. There were times when they would buy something for each of us and surprise us with un-expected gifts, but the overriding principle of work was taught and reinforced. My parents still raised me so that I knew that money came from work—*not* handouts. As an adult, I now see that as a truly life-changing lesson.

Teens should always share the chores around the house, even though as parents of teenagers, you probably won't use chore charts on the fridge to track their jobs. Whether or not you pay your teen a commission for the work he does at home is up to you, but either way, you should encourage him to find work out-side the home. Whether it's running his own lawn care business or working retail, this is when your child will learn how to work in the real world.

An income of *only* home-based commissions gives your teen a safety net. That's both good and bad. It's good in that it rein-forces the work-money connection in a safe environment, but if Mom and Dad are the only "bosses" children know, they won't have the chance to learn other important lessons about working for—and with—other people.

When I was a junior in high school, I had my babysitting experience and Your Integrity Snacks behind me, and I was ready for something new. One of my best friends worked at a store in the mall, and I thought it sounded like fun. So I got a job there during my Christmas break, earning barely above minimum wage. I will never forget getting my first paycheck after working four long days. I was shocked! Just picture a seventeen-year-old girl looking at a pathetically small amount on her paycheck and saying out loud, "You've got to be kidding!" I couldn't believe how small the amount was after so many long days of work. That's when I learned the lesson of "just above minimum wage."

I remember thinking I could have worked as hard babysitting and made double! I finished out the Christmas season and quit.

I learned that I am wired a lot like my dad, and when it comes to work, I'm an entrepreneur at heart. I like working for myself versus a store-type setting. Of course, there's nothing wrong with working retail or at the mall; in fact, that's when I learned about filling out W-2 forms, filing taxes every year, and experiencing the crushing heartache of having the government take a quarter of my paycheck in taxes and Social Security. Those are great lessons for your teens to learn by working outside the home. You may discover that your kids are wired differently. While I didn't care for those types of jobs, my brother and sister both worked in retail through high school and college. Don't put your kids in a box. Allow them to get creative and find a job they enjoy doing.

WORK MATTERS

I've been working in one way or another my whole life, and I admit that sometimes I got a little jealous of my friends whose parents didn't make them work for anything. Now that I'm an adult, though, I have a perspective I didn't have back then. As I travel and talk to young adults, I can tell pretty quickly if they have parents who taught them the value of work or if they have parents who just gave them a twenty every time they asked. If I am talking to teens, I know after asking just a few questions whether or not they're afraid of working hard to meet their money goals. Those teens and young adults who were never taught to work may feel pretty privileged at the time, but I can see the train wreck that's ahead of them. The real world is going to smack them right in the face, and if they don't learn the value of work, they're going to be totally unprepared for it. They will fail.

As a parent, when you don't teach your kids to work, you are not being kind or gracious; you are being irresponsible. It's your responsibility to teach your kids about both money and work. It's not the school's responsibility. It's not the church's responsibility. It's *your* responsibility. Step up to the plate. The direction of your kids' lives—whether or not they're motivated to go out and win—starts with you. You are their biggest supporter and cheerleader. A solid foundation of hard work as kids can completely change their lives as adults—but that will only happen if you, their parents, get engaged and intentional about teaching them *how and why* work matters.

CHAPTER THREE

Spend

When It's Gone, It's Gone

Rachel: "But Dad! Pleeeeeeease! I know I can win this time! I just need a little more money!"

I'm sure the entire theme park heard my passionate plea for help. Looking back, people passing by probably wanted to hand me a few dollars just to shut me up. But no, I was out of luck—and money—for the rest of day. I had to walk around the fantastic Opryland Theme Park for the next six or seven hours in complete torture because I was penniless. And it was all my fault.

Growing up in Nashville, one of my favorite things to do as a little girl was to go to Opryland. It was this awesome amusement park just outside of town that had tons of rides, games, and music-themed attractions. Think of it like a mini Six Flags powered by the spirit of Music City. Our family had season passes, so we went all the time when I was growing up.

This particular trip, I was six years old. I've already told you that by age six, I was working hard at home, getting commissions for the items on my chore chart, and filling my Spend, Save, and Give envelopes with cash. According to my parents, I was making my own money, so I shouldn't just *expect* them to pay for anything special that I wanted to do at the park. Before we left home, Dad had Denise (eight at the time) and me get the money out of our Spend envelopes. He reminded us that we had earned that money ourselves and we had set it aside to spend, so we could spend it however we wanted.

My sister, Denise, had a big, fat Spend envelope because she never really spent any money. Crazy, I know. Anyway, she thought for a minute and said, "You know what? I don't want to spend *all* of my money. I'm just going to take half of it and save the rest." So she carefully counted out exactly half of her money, put it in her pocket, and left the rest in her Spend envelope. I remember thinking, *She's nuts! We're going to Opryland for the whole day! Why on earth wouldn't she take ALL her Spend money and have as much fun as possible?* With that thought ringing in my head, I reached my fingers into my envelope, pulled out every bit of my money, and stuffed it in my pocket. I was six years old and going to my favorite amusement park with a pocket full of cash. The sky was the limit!

As we walked across the parking lot to the front gate, Dad gave us the same little speech he always gave us before entering the park. He reminded us that the money was ours, so we could make our own decisions about what to do with it. Since we had a little money of our own, one of the "Ramsey Rules" was that we kids had to spend our own cash for any extra carnival games we wanted to play.

Now, Denise was probably taking notes at that point. I imagine her hanging on every word, writing it all down, nodding her head and saying, "Yes, yes. That's good stuff, Dad. I think I understand. You don't have to worry about me. I'm going to make this money last and last and last. I'll probably be able to buy all of us dinner on the way home tonight because I'm going to be so careful with my money."

Me? Not so much. I burst through the welcome gates eager and ready to spend some money! I wasn't three steps into the actual park before my eyes landed on the very first game near the entrance. I ran over, slapped some money on the table, and took my turn. I lost. So I put more money down and took another turn. I lost again. And repeat. And repeat. And repeat. Then there was that terrible moment when I reached my hand into my pocket and found nothing there but lint and shattered dreams. I was out of money—at the first game! After only five minutes!

I remember running back over to Mom and Dad, begging for more money. "I know I can win this time! I've got it all fig- ured out!" This, by the way, is why I don't gamble as an adult. It could get very bad, very fast. Anyway, they said no. I even ran over to my sister and said, "Denise! I need some money! Please!" She looked at me like I was out of my mind. By this point, I was crying and even ran back to my mom and said, "Please, Mom! I'll pay you back later!" That's right: I was asking Dave and Sharon Ramsey for a loan. You can imagine how well *that* went over!

Then Dad looked down at me and said something that has stuck with me for more than twenty years. He said, "Rachel, when the money's gone, it's gone. Once you spend it, you can't get it back. If you're already out of money, you're done for the day." And I was. I remember spending the next six hours exploring all the free attractions at the park and watching bitterly while Denise carefully considered whether or not to play certain games. I'm sure I looked pretty pathetic for a while, and I probably drove them crazy with some dramatic whining, but Mom and Dad didn't budge. For the rest of the day, I had to deal with the fact that I had wasted all my money on an impulse. Allowing me to understand that lesson at six years old was an incredible gift my parents gave me.

Dave: It takes tremendous strength and resolve to allow your kids to suffer the consequences of their decisions. They are persuasive, cute, and pushy, so it is really tough not to cave and say to yourself, *Well, they are* only *children.* Certainly there were plenty of times we intentionally bailed out a child who made a dumb mistake. But there were equally as many times when Sharon and I knew if we permitted them to fail while the outcome was under our control, we could keep our hand on the pain thermostat, allowing the temperature to get hot enough to teach the lesson, but not so hot as to do permanent damage. Parents who expect perfection in every decision and allow too much pain are as over the top as "helicopter parents" who hover over their children and never allow them to feel the pain that comes from dumb decisions. Sharon and I tried to strike a balance.

Rachel is the most dramatic of our kids, so she often seemed to turn things into a melodramatic life-or-death discussion. That Opryland experience happened just as she described it, but from our perspective, it was not nearly as dramatic. She simply ran out of money and got no more, end of story. No amount of cuteness, whining, pouting, or persuasion changes the math. You are still broke. And you are broke because you did not control your spending, even after being warned. I meet fifty-four-year-olds who have still not learned this simple lesson.

MONEY HAS LIMITS

Rachel: Money is finite. There is not an infinite supply. That's something a lot of people have trouble remembering these days. In a time when crazy mortgages, car loans, student loans, and credit cards make you believe *anyone* can purchase *anything* at *any time* with no consequences, it's easy to forget that money has limits. Whether your children are six years old at an amusement park or fifty-six years old at a car dealership, they will never win with money until they understand that money can—and often does—*run out*.

To help adults get used to this reality, my dad teaches the envelope system along with the monthly budget. The envelope system is pretty simple: You figure out how much money you can spend in a certain category for the month, and when you get paid, you put that amount in cash into an envelope. So if you budget $500 for food, then you'd put $500 cash in an envelope and write "FOOD" on it. You use only that money for food, and you don't buy any food except with that money. When the envelope is empty, then guess what? You're done buying food. It kind of sounds like what Mom and Dad taught me at Opryland, doesn't it?

That's why I love for parents to use the scaled-down version of the envelope system we talked about in the last chapter with their young children. If you can teach them the limits of money from the beginning, they'll be much less likely to go into all sorts of crazy debt as they get older.

SPENDERS AND SAVERS

Parents, here's a shocker for you: Kids are different. They're unique and act in ways that may not make any sense at all. As your kids grow up, you get the amazing opportunity of watching their little personalities develop. You also get to watch them interact with money. You'll find out pretty quickly whether they are a natural spender or a natural saver. Maybe you read that line and immediately realized that your child is a spender. You might be thinking, *Oh no! I have a spender! She'll never amount to anything and will live in my house the rest of her life! I'm the world's worst parent to have created a little spending monster!*

Okay, take a deep breath, dramatic parents. There's nothing *wrong* with being a spender. You can take my word for it too, because I'm a pretty responsible adult—but I'm *definitely* a natural spender.

I was the kid who couldn't leave the grocery store without a pack of gum or get out of Target without a Slinky or some other little toy simply because I had a dollar in my pocket. If I had any money marked for spending, trust me, I spent it—*fast.* I've always enjoyed the act of spending money. Now, as an adult, that doesn't mean I'm impulsive or irresponsible; it merely means that I've had to recognize that truth about myself and learn how to become a responsible spender. Yes, there is such a thing as a "responsible spender"!

I really want to stress the fact that there's nothing "right" about being a saver, and there's nothing "wrong" with being a spender. This book is absolutely not about how to *change* your little spender into a saver. The goal is to recognize who God uniquely created him to be and to teach him how to handle money, no matter what kind of personality he has. If he's a spender, then let's teach him how to be a *wise* spender (who can also learn to *save* money). If he's a saver, then let's teach him how be a *wise* saver (who can learn to *spend* money).

Let's face it—there are pros and cons to both sides here. Spenders tend to be incredibly generous people, probably because they aren't that concerned with holding on to their money. But spenders can also make impulsive decisions and end up with nothing to show for their hard work. Savers, on the other hand, tend to be naturally patient and more responsible, but they can also become stingy and have trouble spending—or giving—a dime. That's no way to live, either! Bottom line: If you have a spender, that's okay; and if you have a saver, that's okay. Neither is better or worse than the other. But it is important to figure out which type of money personality your child has and direct him toward wise decisions and money habits that are right for him.

Dave: Every one of us has natural strengths and natural weaknesses, and that goes for our tendencies with money, as well. Look for your child's natural strengths and help him or her grow in those areas. Remember, though, that the biggest strength can become a weakness when overdone. A natural saver is great until he never spends and is tight-fisted with giving. A natural spender is great until she finds herself deeply in debt and unable to give. A natural giver is great until there are no savings when a problem arises and there is no personal enjoyment of money. So monitor your children's money strengths and help them keep balance.

Every one of us has natural weaknesses. These are the easy areas to spot and correct with each of your children, but, again, do the correction through the lens of *each child's* uniqueness. If you are a natural saver and your child is a natural spender, be very careful not to make your personality the right one and your child's the wrong one. As a natural spender, the main reason I learned to discipline myself to save was not to become a natural saver. Instead, I save so I have more to give and more to spend. You may have to force children to engage in their area of weakness like you "force" them to brush their teeth, but if you can teach while you are requiring the behavior, you will make a lasting impact.

LEARNING HOW TO SPEND WISELY

Rachel: I think it's pretty clear that six-year-old Rachel wasn't a wise spender that day at Opryland. Even though my parents taught me then and there that money was finite, it was still a lesson I bumped up against for a long time after that. You can't just flip a switch to suddenly turn your children into wise, empowered spenders. Plus, you don't want to go so far that you make your kids think there's something wrong with spending money. There's not! It's like my dad always says, "Money's fun . . . *if you've got some.*" You need to help your kids understand that it's okay to get some nice stuff, as long as they can afford it. There are some specific things you can do to guide your child in this area, and these things are true whether she's a spender or a saver and whether she's six or sixteen.

Be an Example
Your kids are watching you. The most important thing to do when it comes to teaching your children how to be wise spenders is to be a wise spender yourself. I truly believe more is caught

than taught. That means what you *do* is so much more important than what you *say*. If you tell your kids they need to be patient when making a big purchase, but then they see you run off and buy a new flat-screen television on a whim, they will notice the contradiction.

This is true with emotional spending too. Dad and I talk to so many adults who struggle with buying things for the wrong reasons. It's as though they're trying to medicate an emotional need with a new car, purse, TV, or pair of shoes. Let's be honest, ladies, this is a real problem for us sometimes! In a report called *Sheconomics*, researchers studied female spending habits and found that the most common reason a woman goes on a "shopping spree" is to cheer herself up. Almost eight out of ten women surveyed said this is why they shopped. Does it work? Not very well. One-third of that same group reported feeling guilt or shame over a shopping trip within the past week.[1] What makes this so much worse is that your kids are watching you. If you go to the mall or Home Depot every time you're stressed, sad, or emotional, your children will pick up on that. No matter what you *say* about money, they'll get the message loud and clear that the only way to be happy or get over a bad mood is to go out and spend money.

Dave: The phrase "retail therapy" floats off the lips of adults with a self-indulgent, childish smile. When you are so immature that you stand in front of your family and openly proclaim you are going shopping to buy something so you can feel better, you are not cute or funny. You are sending a horrid message to your children. You are saying to them that anytime they feel sad or have problems, buying *stuff* will make it all better. Really? When buying things becomes a coping mechanism, you have truly fallen off the cliff of materialism. You are putting scripts in the minds and spirits of your children that can take them decades of debt to overcome.

Your example is *everything* when teaching your children about money. How many of us as parents have opened our mouths and our mothers' or fathers' words have come out? Your children are going to become a lot like you, so to the extent that you want them to win with money, you better get about the business of winning with money. They will spend like you, save like you, give like you, budget like you, and fight with their future spouse about money . . . like you. Even our facial expressions are learned from our family. What are you modeling?

Rachel: Parents can also get in the habit of buying things for their children out of guilt. This is especially common in single-parent and divorced households. Mom or Dad feels guilty about not being able to spend as much time with their kids as they'd like, so they try to make up for it by buying them a ton of stuff. I've had a lot of teens tell me about their "two Christmases." Occasionally, the parents in those situations actually try to outdo each other, which puts their children in the middle of a weird tug-of-war where everyone loses.

Dave: When one parent attempts to buy love after a divorce, the Disney Dad syndrome sets in. This is frustrating for the other parent who is trying to act like a grown-up and parent with strength. Most family counselors concur that even if you cannot get some agreement in parenting styles with your ex, be careful to never talk trash about him or her, especially in front of your children. The only option you have is to say positive things about the former spouse. Explain to the children that when they are with you, the money lessons will continue because you love them so much and care so much about their future.

In any relationship, remember there is not enough money on the planet to spend or give your way out of guilt. Showering your children with gifts will not erase your feelings of guilt for the divorce or for separating your children from their other parent. When you attempt to buy your children's love, you are being selfish. In an effort to make yourself feel better, you are sending really confusing messages to your children about how life works or doesn't work.

Rachel: Sometimes parents spend money because they feel sorry for their kids. Maybe their daughter loses a soccer game, doesn't make the school play, or gets cut from the band. Who wouldn't want to make her feel better, right? Some parents try to mask the pain and disappointment by buying her things. Parents, please watch your behavior here. We'll talk a lot more about this later when we cover the concept of contentment, but for now, let me remind you that it's up to you to teach your children that spending money won't bring them contentment or fulfillment, and it's not a magic cure for heartache.

Let Your Child Fall Down

I firmly believe that a lot of people make huge, expensive mistakes as adults simply because they were never allowed to make small, inexpensive mistakes when they were kids. Many parents try so hard to protect their children from the pain of hard lessons that they never develop the wisdom and toughness that only come by experiencing failure. Mom and Dad were great in these situations; that day when I blew all my money in five minutes at

Opryland was a perfect example. They didn't say, "Rachel, that's the stupidest thing you could have spent your money on. What a waste." No, that's what control-freak parents say. But they also didn't enable my bad behavior by opening up their wallets and giving me an endless stream of one-dollar bills. They knew I'd just keep throwing that money away at a carnival game I'd never win. Instead, they had a balanced response, and they let me make mistakes and learn from them.

Your children are *going* to learn some hard lessons when it comes to money. They are going to make some bad decisions, maybe some *really* bad decisions. But that's okay. That's how we learn. So it's not a matter of whether or not they *will* make a mistake; it's a question of what *size* mistake they'll make before they learn how to control their spending. As a parent, you've got to let your children fail so they can learn from their mistakes *early*, when the stakes are low. Making a stupid decision with a video game purchase at thirteen isn't quite as devastating as making a stupid car-buying decision at twenty-three.

Teach the Opportunity Cost of Money

Opportunity cost is one of those fancy financial terms that some people choke on. Let me make it easy for you: If you spend all your money on X, then you can't *also* spend that money on Y. This one is pretty easy to explain to your kids. Use an example they care about, such as, "If you buy this video game today, you won't have the money to buy the new game that comes out next month." Sometimes it can be hard for a child to weigh the value of *future* happiness against the immediate thrill of buying something *today*. The key question is, "Will you be as happy about this decision when the new game comes out next month?"

Patience Is a Virtue . . . Really

One of the best ways to avoid a bad purchase is to simply wait overnight. Regardless of how young or old you are, waiting overnight before making a big purchase completely changes the buying decision. That was the rule in our house growing up—even for my parents. Dad's a spender. So early on, Mom and Dad agreed that neither one of them would spend $300 or more without first talking to each other about the purchase and waiting at least overnight so they could sleep on it. I can't tell you how many things Dad *didn't* buy because they didn't seem as important the next morning.

I remember the day Mom suggested this delay technique to me. I was thirteen years old, and Mom and I were out shopping. I saw a shirt that I really liked, but I kept going back and forth on the decision. I'd look at it, hold it up and look in the mirror, then put it back down. This went on for a little while, but I ended up deciding to buy it (with my own hard-earned money, of course). My mom watched all this happen, and she strongly encouraged me to put the shirt on hold overnight so I could think about it some more. I said something like, "But, Mom, I really like it. If I leave it here, someone else will buy it!"

My mom is really wise about this stuff, and she finally convinced me to leave it with the sales clerk—*after* I made the salesperson promise *three separate times* that the shirt would still be there waiting for me the next day. Can you guess what happened? By the time we got home, I had decided that I didn't really want the shirt after all. The next day, I had forgotten all about it. I never went back to get it from the sales clerk who swore she'd hold it for me. It might still be sitting behind a counter somewhere with my name on it.

Fast-forward several years to my junior year of college, when I was in a similar situation. Only this time, Mom was 200 miles away and I was on my own. I was in a store and saw a cardigan that I fell in love with; however, it had a $120 price tag, which definitely made it a major purchase for me. I remembered what Mom and Dad taught me about waiting overnight, so that's what I did. The next day, I decided that I really did want it, so I went back and bought it. I loved it so much that I wore it regularly for the next five years. That was definitely a good purchase for me.

Show your kids that waiting overnight takes the pressure off. It gives you permission to leave the store without the item, and once you leave the store, it's often as though a fog lifts from your mind and you can think clearly again. If you wake up the next day and it still feels like a good purchase (and you can afford it), then it's probably a good purchase for you. Go for it, and enjoy it!

Learning the Art of the Deal

I woke up the morning of my sixth birthday with only one thought: *Will I finally get her today? Were they able to find her?* Later, as I tore open all my birthday presents, I started to get worried. There was no sign of her, and there was only one gift left to open. *Could it be her?* I remember tearing the wrapping paper off that last box, and then my heart skipped a beat. There they were: the two words that give life to six-year-old girls across the country . . . *American Girl.* They had gotten her; I finally owned my own American Girl doll! Could life get any better? Yes, apparently it could.

You see, in the box with my new doll was something I had

never imagined: an American Girl catalog. That little magazine opened my eyes to a whole new world of things that I absolutely had to have. There were other dolls, and those dolls had clothes and accessories and even furniture! I started freaking out, saying, "Mom! Dad! Did you know they have furniture for these dolls? I have to get some. My doll needs somewhere to sit!" They laughed, wished me a happy birthday, and sent me off to play with my new American Girl.

A few hours later, Dad came up to me and told me he had an idea. We got in the car and drove to the local flea market. He said, "Rachel, let's walk around here. If you see any doll furniture that you think would work with your new doll, let me know." So Dave and little Rachel walked around for a while, and soon my eyes landed on some beautiful white wicker doll furniture. I got really excited and pointed it out to Dad. He said, "Okay, I'm going to go over there and talk to the man who's selling it, and we're going to get it for less than he's asking. That's called bargaining. Got it?"

We walked over and Dad struck up a conversation with the guy. Dad had this cool, casual way about him. I was about to burst I was so excited about the furniture, but Dad basically acted like he didn't care if we got it or not. I watched Dad and the seller go back and forth for a few minutes, and then they shook hands. The deal was done! Dad leaned down and said, "He was asking fifty dollars, but we got it for thirty-five. That's a pretty good deal." I remember thinking, *Wow! My dad is the coolest!* That was the day I learned the power of bargaining and negotiating.

Now that I'm an adult, I know that pretty much everywhere else in the world, buyers negotiate prices with sellers on almost

SMART MONEY SMART KIDS

every purchase from food to clothes to houses. But here in America, we tend to walk blindly into a store, pay whatever is on the price tag, and walk out. We never even ask for a deal! Sure, we might do it when we're buying something really big like a car, but otherwise, we just accept the notion that "the price is the price." Most of the time, it's not. Parents, I encourage you to find small ways to show your kids the power of bargaining. My dad taught me that lesson when I was six, and even though I'm a proud spender, I never go into any purchase without looking for—and asking for—a good deal.

Dave: When you model for your child how to negotiate, you are teaching him to face conflict. Negotiating price is a type of conflict. Teaching a child to enter a discussion over price with a win-win spirit teaches him to fight to get the best deal while keeping the other party's dignity in mind.

Also teach your child to make wise purchases by gathering a ton of information. Gathering information about a potential purchase takes the immaturity and the impulse out of the purchase. It emotionally slows down the transaction and makes even a child look at the purchase with more wisdom.

Spenders and Savers Revisited

Rachel: I hope by now you see that there's absolutely nothing wrong with being a spender. Like any other part of your child's personality, it's a natural part of who he is. It is something that you should direct and nurture, not something you have to correct. I'm so grateful my parents gave me the chance to grow into a wise adult spender instead of trying to force me into some mold of how other people think "Dave Ramsey's daughter" should act. I'd go crazy pretending to be a natural saver! Of course, that doesn't mean I don't like saving money. I do . . . *a lot*. So in the next chapter, we'll look at the other side of the coin and discuss how and why to nurture your little savers.

CHAPTER FOUR

Save
Wait for It

Rachel: For two years of my life—from age fourteen to sixteen—I had a single, overriding, obsessive thought. One desire kept me focused. One goal made me willing to give up weekend nights out with my friends. One ambition made the endless hours of babysitting and odd jobs worthwhile. One dream kept me from blowing all my hard-earned money on clothes, music, and movies. Just one thing: a bright yellow Nissan Xterra.

Every time Mom dropped me off at a babysitting job instead of the mall, or Denise and I were driving to Dad's office with food in the car for Your Integrity Snacks instead of heading to the pool on a hot summer day, I dreamed about sixteen-year-old Rachel sitting in the driver's seat, music on, windows down—in her very own car. That SUV was more than just a car for me. It represented freedom. Every time I thought of what my life would be like after my sixteenth birthday, that yellow Xterra was in the background.

Problem was, my parents had been extremely clear with us kids from the beginning: They weren't going to buy each of us a car outright. If we wanted a car when we turned sixteen—or at any age—we had better get to work and save up a pile of cash. That's when this little spender learned to do some *serious* saving.

SAVING IN ACTION

In the last chapter, we focused on spending. That's pretty much the starting point for kids and money. Being able to go into a store and spend their own money is the most powerful way to reinforce the work-money connection we talked about in Chapter 2. But if we stop there, we've got a huge problem. Four-year-olds can get by with the work-money-toy cash flow system; grown-ups can't. If we want to raise young men and women who win with money, we've got to teach them to save.

Behavior Is Key

We are definitely not a nation of savers today. A recent survey by the National Foundation for Credit Counseling found that 64 percent of Americans couldn't even cover a $1,000 emergency with cash.[1] In real-life terms, that means they couldn't pull together enough money for a single mortgage payment, or maybe even a month's worth of groceries for their family, without borrowing money. Another study from Bankrate.com found that one in four Americans does not have a *single penny* saved.[2] Clearly, this situation is a complete disaster. So why do millions of Americans accept it as a way of life?

Not surprisingly, research shows that adults are failing with money because of the money habits they developed as children. CNN recently reported on a study of college students at the University of Illinois at Urbana-Champaign. The researchers found one striking similarity among students who consistently demonstrated good financial skills. According to the report, "Nearly all said their parents had gotten them into the habit of saving as young children, suggesting saving is a behavior that comes from experience, not knowledge."[3] That just backs up what my dad's been saying for more than twenty years: Personal finance is 80 percent *behavior*; it's only 20 percent *head knowledge*.

Dave: After decades of coaching adults who have messed up financially, as well as those who have become wealthy, I am more convinced than ever that behavior is the primary indicator of successful wealth building. If you want to know if someone will win with money, all you have to do is look at his behavior and the character that drives that behavior. An adult's ability to work well with people, have extreme integrity, and display emotional and spiritual maturity are key to building wealth and keeping it. Great talent might cause someone to get rich, but it usually flames out if he doesn't know how to behave like a grown-up.

When you repeatedly teach your child proper spending, saving, and giving behaviors until those behaviors become character traits, you are ensuring the future success of your child. When a kid saves money, it is not a mathematical event; it is a maturity event that gives dignity. When a kid buys something with money he or she has saved, it is not merely a financial transaction; you are watching poise, confidence, and maturity develop right before your eyes. When you grow great behaviors and character traits in your children, you are really teaching them how to win at life.

Rachel: Saving money can be hard to do no matter how old (or young) you are. So teaching your kids how and why to save money as early as possible will give them a major head start. You also have to give them the opportunity to *experience* saving money. Information alone rarely changes our behaviors; instead, we tend to learn the most by *doing* or *experiencing* something. I'm meeting more and more teens and young adults who have trouble saving money simply because they never had to do it, and they never really saw their parents do it. It was something their family never made a priority.

As a parent, you need to understand that your children are in the best position of their lives to learn about saving money. Young kids living at home are usually in the most financially secure position they'll ever be in. Give them the opportunity to experience saving in action.

Saving Teaches Patience

Kids aren't always naturally patient people. Shocking, I know. One of the most terrifying moments for many parents is getting to a restaurant and hearing the phrase, "We've got a forty-five-minute wait." When you're five, forty-five minutes is an eternity! Those moments, however—as painful as they can be for kids *and* parents—are important. They teach children how to wait for something fun, and that's a huge lesson in today's world.

We live in a culture of instant gratification. We don't want to wait for anything anymore, and technology keeps feeding our get-it-now attitudes. You can check the weather, make dinner reservations, order a pair of shoes, and send a picture to a friend, all while walking into work. When it comes to buying stuff, marketing, advertising, pop culture, and "easy payments" have all come together to create a perfect storm that's turned us into a ridiculously fast-paced, instant gratification society. We can have almost anything we want, any time we want, whether or not we have the money to pay for it.

But you are a lot more cautious about a purchase if you take the time to actually save up and pay cash for it. When that happens, you're learning delayed gratification. As that becomes part of your personality, you understand that you can't have everything you want right when you want it. This is a great lesson to learn early in life. From a child's perspective, saving means it will take a few *weeks* to have enough money for that special toy. As children grow up, they'll understand that it will take several *months* to save for a car, and probably a few *years* to save for that down payment on a house.

Having your children save up for big purchases—and giving them the chance to see you do the same—teaches invaluable lessons in patience and goal setting. Plus, slowing down and saving up to buy things teaches them to make wiser, less spontaneous purchasing decisions. This was definitely a lesson I needed to learn when I was fourteen and saving for my dream car. Most importantly, though, learning how and why to save money over time helps prevent the horrible entitlement mentality that many kids have today. Simply teaching kids how to save money from a young age can completely prevent that "I deserve it" attitude from ever creeping in to their mindset.

Remember, your children are watching you. If they see you work hard, set a goal, save up, and pay cash for a big purchase, that's probably what they'll do too. On the other hand, if they see you put a big purchase on a credit card and then stress out about paying the bill for the next few months, then that's how they'll think money works. The stakes get much higher as your kids get older. The opportunity to learn and witness the discipline of saving at a young age can be one of the greatest tools you pass on to your children.

SAVING FOR PURCHASES: AGES SIX TO THIRTEEN

My dad has always taught that people need to save for three reasons: first, an emergency fund, then purchases, and then wealth building. I completely agree with that, but when you're dealing with children, you need to change up the order a bit. Like we've said, the best opportunity you'll have to start teaching your young children about money is in their purchases. So that's where we'll start.

Introducing Saving

When your kids are ages six to thirteen, they can start to grasp the concept of saving. Remember, up until age six, all the money was essentially marked for spending in the big clear plastic container. Now they have envelopes to allocate some for spending, saving, and giving. When they move into "big kid" envelopes at age six, you can really play this up. Make sure they understand this is a big deal! Also be sure to add more jobs to the chore chart to give them more opportunities to make money. If you keep their commissions the same but start dividing their money into three envelopes instead of just one big Spend bucket, you could accidentally demotivate them.

In my family, Mom and Dad helped us allocate the money

across our envelopes. Early on, I got five dollars a week for my chores, and two dollars of that went into my Save envelope. So, as a rough guideline, you might try marking 40 percent of your child's commissions for saving. That's not a hard rule; you should use whatever works for your family. Just remember—we're not talking about saving for retirement here. For ages six to thirteen, the Save envelope is really just a bigger, slower Spend envelope. This is how kids will be able to buy a toy themselves, so be careful not to give the impression that the Save envelope is a black hole where their hard-earned money disappears!

Savings and Goal Setting

It's a great feeling to set a purchasing goal, work hard over time to reach it, and then actually buy the item. That feeling is magnified when it comes to your kids saving for their own purchases. There is an enormous sense of accomplishment for a child when he walks into a store and makes a significant purchase with money that he earned himself. Something inside him lights up and shouts, *Look what I just did!* Having Mom and Dad alongside, cheering him on, adds to the thrill because he's so proud of what he's achieved.

Help your child pick out a toy, movie, video game, or other item that he wants, and if it's in a reasonable, attainable price range, encourage him to set a savings goal to buy it. Remember, kids are incredibly visual, so print a picture of the item and tape it to the refrigerator next to his chore chart. As he works toward it for the next few weeks, ask him how it's going. Knowing that you are excited for him can keep his motivation level high as he puts money into the Save envelope every week.

Then, once he reaches the goal, make it a celebratory trip when going to the store to buy the item. Occasionally, if you're able, you might even add a special surprise to the purchase. For example, if your son saves up and buys a video game, maybe you could surprise him with a new controller. Or if the item he wants is really out of his price range, you could offer to match his savings on a big goal. You shouldn't do this every time, but sometimes it can be a fun way to celebrate with and encourage your child.

A friend recently told me about a six-year-old he knows named Drew who set a major savings goal—and completely dominated it! Drew had spent some time playing with an iPad Mini in a store while his parents shopped. He decided then and there that he really wanted one. His parents saw that he was serious, so they sat down and explained what a big goal it was and how long it would probably take to save enough money for the purchase. Drew was so determined that his parents knew they needed to make this a major learning experience. They told him they'd match his savings dollar for dollar on an iPad, but he'd have to come up with his half on his own. Being only six, Drew wasn't making a fortune in commissions, but he got creative and found new ways to make money. When his birthday rolled around, he told his whole extended family that he only wanted money for the iPad. That meant no toys, games, or other gifts. For a six-year-old, not getting a single toy on your birthday is a big deal, but he was focused on his goal.

Drew was still seventy dollars short one night when his parents saw that the local retail store had discounted the iPad Mini he wanted. They counted up his money, applied the match, and Drew had just enough money to go to the store and bring his iPad home! Can you even imagine how proud that little boy must have been? At six years old, he was able to make a purchase that many adults can't afford. And he did it through hard work and patience—and with some encouragement from parents who really get it.

Parents' Role in Purchases

Dave: One of the most important reasons you teach your children to spend wisely and save is to give them life skills. The actual transaction should not matter; what's important is the exercise itself and the lesson learned. So as you are leading them in purchases, you will have to decide when to bail them out as an act of grace, and when to hold strong and walk out of the store with a disappointed child. Be an advisor to them, teaching them about quality, negotiating, and gathering information. Sometimes you can let them buy the cheap toy even after you warned them it may break the first day they own it. When the toy breaks just as you predicted, remind them that you love them and that they can trust you on future purchases. At other times, you will have to step in and put your foot down to protect them from themselves.

Under no circumstances do you give up your right to parent and make a ruling simply because your child earned some money somewhere. "It's my money, and I can buy whatever I want" was not a statement that we allowed in our family. Children cannot be allowed to buy things or do things you don't approve of just because they earned some money. If your kids are allowed to do whatever they want, you are not a parent; you are a zoo keeper. Obviously, if a teen wants to spend his or her money on cocaine, you are not going to allow that. Hopefully, drugs won't be a problem in your home, but you will have to make parental—not financial—decisions on proper clothing, tattoos, piercings, trips with questionable friends, cell phone usage, and much, much more. In those cases, you will have to decide for your household where the line is. Just because you are creating teachable money moments does not mean you resign your role as parent. You are still in charge.

Many years ago, one of the Ramsey girls was saving for a Celebration Barbie. When we got to the store with her little jar of money, she wasn't even close to having the full amount. It was very hard as a dad to look at that little girl and not bail her out and buy the Barbie. Even though she had a closet full of Barbies, this was the desired purchase. I helped her with the math, showing her that she had five dollars and the purchase was twenty-five dollars. Then I gave her the option of buying something less expensive or leaving the store and coming back after saving a while longer. Before you think I am a tough ogre, this was not a big goal that had been discussed and systematically saved for over many months. This was simply a trip to the store that didn't work out. If she had been close after diligently working a long time, I would have chipped in a little. But the character built by understanding that Celebration Barbie was not in her budget was worth more on that particular trip. Rather than going home with Celebration Barbie, we went home with "Sorta Had a Party Barbie."

Grace vs. Legalism

Rachel: I definitely agree that parents shouldn't *always* step in and rescue their child when she doesn't have enough money for her purchase, but please—*please*—don't go overboard with this. I spoke to a group of moms a while back, and one of the women came up to the front afterward and said, "Rachel, our family does everything you and Dave teach. My ten-year-old son is on the envelope system, and he saved up $300 for a PlayStation." I thought that was going to be the end of the story. I mean, that's incredible! I was about to give her a hug and tell her what a fantastic job she was doing with her son. Seriously, a ten-year-old saved $300!

Then she continued, "But he forgot about tax. When we were at the store, they rang it up and the tax made it more than he had. So we left the store without it." I could tell she was actually proud of herself in that situation. I think she was expecting me to congratulate her on taking such a hard stance with her son's big purchase. Well . . . she was wrong.

My jaw dropped, and I thought, *What? Your ten-year-old worked and saved $300! You pay the tax! Are you kidding me?* See, that's exactly the kind of behavior you want to reward in your children. If you have a child that age saving that much money, making big financial goals and actually reaching them no matter how long it takes, you want him to remember that as a positive experience. Don't rain on his parade by making him go home empty-handed!

When you're trying to decide whether or not to step in and help, the bottom line is this: Too many rules is legalistic, but too much grace is enabling. You want to encourage and reward their hard work, but you don't want to make them think you'll always be there with a handout if they fall short. You've got to maintain that balance, especially for ages six to thirteen.

SAVING FOR PURCHASES: AGES FOURTEEN TO COLLEGE

Teenagers have a whole new set of savings goals. Sure, they're still buying some "toys," but those look more like electronic gadgets or purses. On top of that, the normal expenses of teenage life begin to resemble adult life. They start going out with their friends, going out on dates, buying gas, paying cell phone bills, and generally needing more money.

Parents, your little baby is growing up—and so are her financial needs. That means it's time to get more focused and intentional than ever about saving money.

We already explored what work looks like for teenagers, so we know where the money is coming from. Now let's talk about where that money is going. There are basically two huge expenses that most American teens face these days: buying a car and paying for college. How to go to college debt free is such a big deal that we'll devote a full chapter to it later. For now, let's talk about how your teen can buy her first car.

The 401DAVE Plan

Mom and Dad told us kids from a young age that there wouldn't be a brand-new car sitting in the driveway with a big red bow on it on our sixteenth birthday. They told us they would pay for half the cost of our cars when we got our driver's licenses. Whatever amount of money we saved, Mom and Dad agreed to match it. Dad liked to call this his "401DAVE" plan. So if we wanted a car, it was up to us to save for it. I remember when Denise turned sixteen, all three of us kids held our breath to see what Mom and Dad would do. I knew they always kept their word, but at the same time I held out this hope that when the time came, they'd surprise us by telling us to keep our hard-earned money while they paid for the whole car themselves. I could just imagine Dad saying, "Great job, Denise! I'm so proud of you for saving so much money. I'll let you in on a little secret, though. We planned on buying you a car all along! Happy birthday!"

See, I was fourteen at the time and had some money saved,

but not enough for a car. Maybe a nice bike, but definitely not a car. And honestly, the thought of saving up that much money seemed impossible. They had to be joking, right? I mean, who expects a sixteen-year-old to have $2,000 or $4,000 or $6,000 on hand for a car? The more I thought about it, the more I became convinced that this was just one of those "Dave Ramsey teachable moments," and he wasn't really going to go through with it.

When Denise turned sixteen and got her driver's license, they counted up everything she had saved, and it added up to $4,500. Mom and Dad congratulated her, told her what a great job she had done, and then . . . they matched it. Dollar for dollar. Just like they said they would. There was no car in the driveway and no shiny set of new car keys in a tiny box beside her birthday cake that night. My parents did what they promised, which meant Denise went car shopping with a total of $9,000 to spend. That sent a clear message to Daniel and me: 401DAVE was real, and the kind of car we would get depended entirely on how hard we were willing to work and how disciplined we were about saving.

Saving Money Won't Kill Your Kids

I'm not going to lie: I really didn't like Denise's car very much. Sure, it was in good shape and it got us back and forth to the store for our frequent restocking trips for Your Integrity Snacks, but it wasn't what I wanted to end up with. Simply put: I wanted a better car than my sister had. That's when the dream of the magical yellow Xterra started growing in my fourteen-year-old mind. The problem was, I still thought it was impossible for me to save up that much money. I was fourteen when Denise turned sixteen, so that meant I had only two more years to save. There was no way I could do it!

So I did the only thing I could think of: I created a full

PowerPoint presentation for my parents, outlining exactly why it would be *crazy* to make me save up for a car. I got everything ready, and then I called them into the living room for my little speech. I went through—in great detail—all of the bad things that could happen if I had to save enough money for half of my car. For example, I told them in a serious tone how much my schoolwork would suffer if I had to spend so much time working. I needed to focus on my education. If I fell far enough behind at school because of part-time work, I would fail out of high school. Then I'd never be able to go to college, and I'd end up working in a fast-food restaurant my whole life! To drive that last point home, I added in several slides with logos from Burger King, Taco Bell, and McDonald's.

Then the presentation got even more serious. I passionately explained how worrying about saving that much money would put a huge amount of stress on me, which would endanger my health. *My health!* If I worked that hard, I wouldn't get enough sleep and would end up physically ill. That would lead to a weakened immune system, which would eventually lead to my death! For the big finish, I cried, "How can you possibly put me—a happy, healthy young teenager—in that kind of jeopardy? *I am your own daughter!*" Cue the tears.

I'm sorry, did I say "tears"? I must have meant "cue the laughter," because that's the only reaction I got. Mom and Dad looked at each other, totally cracking up as they got up from the couch. As they walked out of my failed sales presentation, Dad just looked down and said, "You get points for being creative, Rachel. But you better get to work." So . . . I did.

Dave: Yeah, when drama doesn't work, you have to try *working*!

Double or Nothing

Rachel: For the next two years, I got serious about saving money. I had been a spender all my life, and for the first time, I started to analyze every little nickel-and-dime purchase I made. Because of the match, I knew that all of my spending and saving decisions were doubled. If I spent fifty dollars of my babysitting money on clothes, I'd have $100 less for my car. Or if I turned down a thirty-dollar babysitting job one night, it would really cost me sixty dollars when it was time to buy the car. That realization alone gave me a ton of incentive to not only keep saving, but to also avoid spending.

After two long years of saving and sacrificing, the day finally came. On my sixteenth birthday, I had a total of $8,000 saved up—*before* the match. That meant I had $16,000 to spend on a car! Not bad for a tenth-grader. In fact, I felt really empowered. I knew that Xterra would be mine!

Revising the Dream

When the day finally came to go car shopping, I thought, *This will be easy. I know exactly what I want, they have it in stock, and I can afford it. This won't take long at all—and I am going to leave here with my own car!* But once I got the SUV out on the road for a test drive, two years' worth of expectation and excitement quickly drained out of me. I didn't like it. I didn't like the way it drove. It didn't feel right. *What? How could this be happening?* I thought. I couldn't talk myself into it. The magnificent yellow Xterra of my dreams was gone. I had to start the car search over from scratch.

This created a whole new learning opportunity for Dad and me that I never expected. It gave us the chance to talk about what a big decision it was to select the right car. Dad said, "Rachel, this is how you learn patience. As you grow up, you'll discover that a lot of things you *think* you want actually turn out to be not as great as you expected. A car is one of the biggest purchases you'll ever make, so let's take a step back, catch our breath, and think about what you really want. This is *not* the time to get impulsive just because the Xterra didn't work out. That's how people end up making terrible decisions that haunt them for years. I don't want that to happen to you after you worked so hard to save this money."

Looking back, that lesson in the car lot was almost as valuable to me as the whole car-saving experience. With a clean slate and $16,000 to spend, Dad and I started a new car search. Along the way, I got to experience the power of cash in negotiating. Putting a little bit down and making monthly payments for five years doesn't give you much leverage when you're standing face to face with a car dealer. But standing at the front of a car you like and waving $16,000 under the dealer's nose? Yeah, that gets you a bargain.

Lessons Learned

When all was said and done, I ended up with a beautiful black BMW 323. It was used, of course, but in great condition. It served me well for several years, and I loved that car. Because I had worked so hard for it for so long, I drove it a lot differently than my friends who had a car handed to them. I knew that car was *mine*, not because I *owned* it, but because I *earned* it. That made me appreciate it and care for it on a level I never expected.

I learned a lot of other lessons through my two-year car-saving drama, too. The main thing that stuck with me is that even twelve- or thirteen-year-old children are capable of setting—and achieving—enormous financial goals. I think back to when I was fourteen, making a case to my parents about how impossible it would be for me to save that much money. I didn't believe I could do it. Fortunately for me, my parents knew I could. They never doubted what I could accomplish if I would set my mind on the goal. Their confidence in my abilities frustrated me at the time, but it's so precious to me now.

I also learned that hard work never killed anyone—not even someone in high school. I didn't have any trouble getting good grades and really enjoying my high school years while I was working hard for my car money. I figured out how to manage my time so I could do everything I wanted and needed to do.

All of the lessons I learned during those years—the power of cash, the importance of wise decision making, and the discipline of working toward a big goal—are major parts of the woman I've become. And I owe it all to 401DAVE. Go figure.

Dave: We are so proud of all three of our children for working, saving, making the most of the match, and making wise purchases on cars. We certainly had the money to write a check and buy each of them a brand-new car on their sixteenth birthday, but that perpetuates the entitlement mentality.

Not everyone is able to match. You may match part, but maybe not dollar for dollar. Perhaps others can provide income opportunities for your children to earn the money for a car. Because my parents were in the real estate business, they were able to get me jobs painting and fixing up houses when I was fifteen, and that helped me earn enough for my first car.

A car purchase—or any other item your child saves for—gives you the opportunity for multiple teachable moments. Rachel learned many lessons with her car purchase. First, she learned she couldn't "sell" her way into a car—drama is not interchangeable with money. Second, she learned more about the value of working hard. Third, she grew up, because saving money requires emotional maturity. Delaying pleasure is one definition of maturity. Adults devise a plan and follow it; children do what feels good. So Rachel grew up a lot while saving for her car. Fourth, she learned goal setting. Fifth, she learned to gather information before buying something, especially after the test drive in the yellow Xterra didn't go so well. I remember watching her body language change as she made the decision to walk away from the very car she thought she had worked so hard for. I watched a girl move toward womanhood before my eyes as she straightened her posture, threw her shoulders back, and walked away toward a better car. None of this would have happened if Sharon and I had simply bought Rachel a car.

One other note: If you're thinking about doing a matching funds arrangement like we did, I encourage you to put a cap on *how much* you'll match. You'll see why this is important in the next chapter when you hear how well my son did with his 401DAVE.

SAVING FOR EMERGENCIES
AND WEALTH BUILDING

Rachel: We said teens and adults need to save money for three reasons: purchases, an emergency fund, and wealth building. We've covered purchases pretty well, but the other two reasons—emergencies and wealth—can be a tougher sell for your teen. Getting a teenager excited about saving for emergencies can be a difficult task.

What's an Emergency?

Once your child is in high school, I recommend he saves up a $500 emergency fund. Sure, you as the parent will be there to cover any *real* emergencies like health scares, injuries, and major accidents. But teenagers have teen-sized emergencies pop up all the time that they should be prepared to handle. For example, a cracked cell phone may not make it on your list of critical emergencies, but losing the ability to text could be the end of the world for your teen. Of course, you could replace a broken phone (and there's nothing wrong with that), but if your son comes to you with his third broken phone in less than a year, he may need to feel that responsibility himself. If he has to buy his own replacement phone, maybe he'll be a little more careful . . . and invest in a thick case for it, too.

I got a flat tire once in high school, and I vividly remember the feeling of pulling the money out of my own savings account to fix it. It's amazing how those moments changed my view of money and my stuff. It wasn't just about ownership; it was about responsibility. I took better care of my things when I knew I carried much of the financial responsibility for them. Of course, emergencies didn't happen very often. I can count on one hand how many times I had to dip into my own emergency fund. But having that money set aside in the bank gave me a feeling of confidence and independence. I knew that if something happened, I could probably cover it. That's a feeling a lot of adults don't have, but my parents instilled it in me when I was a teenager.

As the parent, you're training your children to be competent adults—and adults need to be prepared for emergencies. So teach your kids to save up a $500 emergency fund in high school, and don't be scared to let them use it for their own emergencies from time to time.

Setting an Example of Saving

Dave: Parents, when your hot water heater goes out, your children are watching your reaction. If you go into freak-out, drama mode every time there is an emergency because you are broke and have no emergency fund, then your children will learn that emergencies mean panic and worry. If instead, you simply write a check and fix the hot water heater, the children will feel emotionally secure because the household is stable, and they will also observe how important a rainy-day fund is. To make sure your children are learning, talk through the event and discuss why you were not freaked out.

Many of us grew up knowing about our grandparents who always had rainy-day funds. One lady in *Financial Peace University* told me her grandmother always paid for problems out of her G.O.K. fund—her "God Only Knows" fund. Lesson observed and lesson learned.

Never Too Young for Wealth Building

Rachel: When I was growing up, my parents kept me focused on the basics. I had an emergency fund, I never used debt, I paid cash for my car, and I made sure my college education was covered. If your child has those bases covered, she's doing great! But don't be afraid to push it just a bit further and start explaining how investing and wealth building works. Even if she doesn't put it into practice right away, laying that groundwork early on can change what she does with that first paycheck out of college.

I was in high school when I first asked my dad how a mutual fund works. I'll admit I didn't get it at first, but after several conversations, I finally understood. He even explained to me what compound interest was and how important it is to start investing early. It's amazing to me that many young adults I meet have no idea how investing works. These are working adults who are earning real money and squandering years of compound interest because they don't grasp the urgency of investing early in life. They're losing literally hundreds of thousands of future dollars because they lack the training and information.

Don't miss your chance! You have the power *today* to set your child up to be a millionaire by giving him this knowledge. And in doing that, you can completely change your family's financial legacy.

Dave: Teaching small children about mutual funds or compound interest is ridiculous unless you are raising a genius. Nevertheless, from time to time as they are growing up, you can show your children the file where you keep their college saving investment statement. Then when they are around twelve years old, pull the statement out and let them do the simple math to see the future value of the account.

Sharon and I kept our children's college investment funds an occasional topic of conversation as they grew up. First, this showed them that college attendance was assumed at our house and that we were saving to give them a better life. Second, using the actual financial terms provided a quick teachable moment for our twelve-year-old. Once they were in high school, I sat down with them and explained what a mutual fund is and how it works. Honestly, I didn't expect all the details to stick, and they didn't, but the overarching discussion did—that college and investing are a natural part of life. So for my grown kids today, they just assume that they should be investing—and as they actually do it, they relearn the details for themselves.

Long-term investing is important, but your teenager has a couple of more urgent savings goals: buying a car and paying for college. In Chapter 6, we'll walk through the five things your teen should do with his money before long-term wealth building enters the picture. If you want to know more about long-term investing in general, be sure to check out daveramsey.com for plenty of information, tools, and resources.

SAVING FOR LIFE

Rachel: Learning how and why to save money is one of the most fundamental financial disciplines there is. I can't think of a better way to set your child up for lifelong success than to simply teach him how to save. It's not always easy, and it certainly isn't always fun. But knowing how to save, delay gratification, set goals and priorities, make huge purchases with cash instead of debt, cover emergencies, and prepare for long-term investing is critical for any young man or woman leaving home for the first time. These are all lessons you can teach your children *today*, no matter how old they are or where you're starting from.

CHAPTER FIVE

Give

It's Not Yours Anyway

Dave: As far back as I can remember, I have been driven to reach certain goals. My parents gave me the wonderful gift of believing I could do anything I set my mind to if I only worked hard enough. So as a young man I set my mind to the gathering of "stuff." Some people call that materialism, and there might be some truth to that, but all I know is that I wanted some *stuff*. Making money was simply a means for me to live the good life, because, after all, it *was* all about me. Or, did I mention that already?

Since making and having money was simply an exercise in self-indulgence, I was more than a little self-centered. Then in my early twenties, I met God. I met Him in a radical, life-changing way, and after He entered my life, He began reshaping my selfish heart into the heart of a giver. He has been working on that young selfish guy ever since. I began to learn and understand what Christians call "stewardship."

Stewardship is really not a Christian word, but an Old English word from around the time of the King James translation of the Bible. The word in feudal economic times described a person who didn't own anything, but managed the affairs of the lord of the realm. This manager's title was "steward." He had a nice house, beautiful clothes, and fine food, but it wasn't really his. He enjoyed all of the benefits of the lord's wealth, but he felt no sense of ownership over it. Similar to those medieval stewards, when we realize we are simply managing someone else's money, it changes our focus.

For instance, it is easier to give away other people's money than it is to give away your own money. The first and most important lesson about money that Sharon and I taught our children is that money is not theirs. As a family of faith, we believe that God owns everything, and we are asked to manage it for Him. We don't own it, which makes it easier to give.

Recently we made a $10,000 donation from our company to a radiothon. I don't know where you grew up, but where I come from, that is a lot of money. I asked my controller to write the $10,000 check, and she did not hesitate. It was not hard at all for her to give away my money. Sure, it was a little harder for me than it was for her, but it wasn't really that hard for me either. She knew the money wasn't hers, and I knew the money wasn't mine. It was God's, and as a steward, I was just doing what the Owner told me to do.

If you want children who are less selfish; if you want children who view wealth as a responsibility, not a meal ticket; if you want children who look at the future as a bright place; if you want children who function with a spirit of abundance rather than a spirit of lack, then you must teach them that they don't *own* money—they are simply managers, or stewards of it.

CURING THE ME MENTALITY

Rachel: It's always funny for me to hear Dad talk about how hard it was for him to learn how to give. The truth is, giving has been a big part of our family for as long as I can remember. The thought that there was a twenty-something version of Dad back then who *didn't* give is hard for me to imagine. It really demonstrates how powerful these principles are and how they can totally transform you at any age. My whole life, I have only known Mom and Dad as outrageous givers. That doesn't mean they give money to every single ministry or charity that asks for donations, and it certainly doesn't mean that they've always gotten it right. Trust me, they've made *plenty* of mistakes, even after they learned these lessons. Hey, I've made plenty of mistakes myself, and I've been living by these principles since I was born! No family—not even ours—gets this stuff right every time.

What Mom and Dad did get right, though, was providing a solid foundation of generosity for my sister, brother, and me. That doesn't mean I never struggle with a selfish thought—I'm a fun-loving natural spender, remember? It just means that even when I get distracted by selfish things, I can always go back to the starting point for my family: giving. Unfortunately, it's a counter-culture message that many young people just don't get.

Generation Me

As I travel across the country speaking to teens, I meet a lot of sweet, responsible, hard-working kids. But I have encountered a lot of self-centered ones too. And because of the work I do, I've come across studies that examine the self-consumed nature of this generation sometimes called "Generation Me." One recent study from

Journal of Personality and Social Psychology found that "compared to Boomers, Millennials [those born between the early 1980s and the early 2000s] were less likely to have donated to charities, less likely to want a job worthwhile to society or that would help others, and less likely to agree they would eat differently if it meant more food for the starving. They were less likely to want to work in a social service organization or become a social worker, and were less likely to express empathy for outgroups."[1] That's a tragedy! And the tragedy isn't just that they aren't likely to give to people in need or to worthy causes; it's that they'll never experience the power of giving in their own lives.

Having a selfish mentality is a big obstacle for a lot of people. It's definitely something your kids either already struggle with or will face one day. That's because they are growing up in a culture that is obsessed with me, me, me. *How do I look? How do I feel? What can I buy myself? What makes me happy? What makes me comfortable? What can I do to make life easier for myself?* I'm not saying that every young person in America is selfish and greedy, but let's face it: The act of giving isn't always the first thing they think about. But when your kids grow up in a house where giving is a priority, they start to see *themselves* differently because they see *other people* differently. Other people become significant, and doing things for others becomes a priority. The antidote for selfishness isn't a theory; it's an action, and that action is giving.

Selfish People Stink

Dave: Have you ever met someone and after being around him you felt like you needed a shower? That sliminess, that scent of scum, is the smell of a selfish person. Selfish people are transactional rather than relational. They are involved in every exchange only for what they can get out of it.

Selfish people have a spiritual smell to them. There is a reason for that smell: They never give. People who never give are stopped-up—nothing flows through—and anything that is stopped-up eventually begins to stink. The Dead Sea is the largest body of water with no life. There is no life because water flows from the Jordan River into the Dead Sea and just stays there—there are no streams for water to flow out. Similarly, a pond with no outlet will grow scum on its surface. People's spirits are the same way. A person who doesn't give is really dead; there's not much spiritual life flowing through him.

TEACH GIVING BY EXAMPLE

Rachel: We have said several times that your children are watching you. That's true in how you work, how you spend, and how you save, but it may never be truer than it is in how you give. If your children never see you give to someone or something else, then they'll never learn how to do it themselves. Even worse, if you try to *tell* them to give without *showing* them what giving looks like, then the whole message about giving, spending, and saving will be lost because you'll be doing one thing but saying another.

More Is Caught Than Taught

I truly believe more is caught than taught . . . that what your kids *see you do* is a lot more powerful than what they *hear you say*. Words can be strong, but actions are stronger. The strongest impact on children, though, is when they hear and see a consistent message from their parents. When the parents' words and actions come together, it forms a powerful statement about that family's value system.

I've told you that church was important to my family, and my parents have tithed to the church my entire life. That wasn't just something we talked about at home; it was something I got to see them do on a weekly basis. Every Sunday, I watched Mom and Dad put a folded check in the red velvet offering bag as people passed it down the pew. That image is burned in my mind even now as an adult. No matter how much we were struggling financially, no matter how big or small Dad's paycheck was, Dad and Mom put a check in that bag every single week. Seeing that consistent act of giving made it so natural for Denise, Daniel, and me when our parents started talking to us about our own Give envelopes. Because we watched Mom and Dad give, we knew that one of our family values was to give a percentage of whatever money we made. So even as kids, that's what we did.

Many parents miss this opportunity not because they aren't giving, but because they aren't being intentional about letting their kids *see* them give. With online banking, it is so easy to do all your giving in two or three clicks while you're doing the budget. I'll be the first to admit that I love giving online. It's quick and convenient. But if you're a parent, online giving robs you of a chance to make a powerful visual statement to your kids. Even if you're an online banker like me, I suggest digging out the old-fashioned checkbook once a week for your giving. Let your kids watch you write out the check, and use the opportunity to reinforce why you give. If you're a Christian and you're writing out a check for your tithe, remind them what the tithe is (10 percent of your income given to the local church) and why it's important. If you're writing a check to a charity or nonprofit, talk to your child about the organization and how your contribution will serve or support them. Help them make the mental and emotional connection between the money and the people it's going to help.

You may not want your child to see the dollar amount that you're giving, especially if you're giving 10 percent of your income. That's fine. I never knew the amount on the checks my parents placed in the offering bag, but I never doubted that it was 10 percent of whatever Dad made that week. Seeing them put the check in the bag was the weekly exclamation point on the ongoing discussion our family had about giving. The amount really wasn't important to me as a child. The real value was in seeing how Mom and Dad's actions lined up with their words. All this may seem like a hassle, but providing your child the chance to see you give will make a huge impact. All these years later, the image of my parents dropping that check in the red velvet bag still goes through my mind every time I give my own tithe.

401DAVE on Steroids

If you do these things when your kids are younger, you may be shocked to see what happens as they grow and mature. The lessons you're teaching them about saving and giving may seem "cute" when they're six years old, but remember, you're laying a foundation here. You never know what they will build on that foundation as their opportunities (and income) grow over time. I can't imagine a better example of this than what I saw my brother, Daniel, do when he was only sixteen.

I've told you about Dad's 401DAVE plan for how Denise, Daniel, and I saved for and bought our cars. Basically, Mom and Dad matched our car savings dollar for dollar. All three of us got that message at the same time, and Daniel was the youngest. He was ten years old when he saw our parents match Denise's car savings, which meant he had six years to save up for his car. He did all sorts of odd jobs, worked at Dad's office building during the summers, and even painted two five-story stairwells one year. Over those six years, my brother earned and saved an impressive $12,000 for a car—and that was before the match!

Dad sat him down one night before Daniel turned sixteen and said, "Listen, buddy, I am so proud of you. You have done an amazing job saving, and we're going to match your savings just like we promised. But as a dad, I can't let my sixteen-year-old kid buy a $24,000 car. There's no way." It worked out all right, because Daniel had his eye on a great $14,000 Jeep anyway. But that meant Daniel had another $10,000 left over just sitting in the bank.

Later that year, Daniel took a mission trip to Peru and developed a huge heart both for missions and for the area where he served. When he got home from that trip, he talked about how much that experience had impacted his life. Not long after that, there was a massive earthquake in Peru near the town where Daniel had served. When he heard about it, Daniel felt a heavy burden to do something. He told Dad that he wanted to give the rest of his car money to the disaster recovery efforts in Peru. Did you catch that? A sixteen-year-old kid wanted to give $10,000 of his own hard-earned money to a community in another part of the world! Who does that?

That really caught Dad off guard. He said, "Daniel, are you sure you want to do that? I mean, you'll be heading to college soon, and you'll want to do all sorts of things over the next few years."

Daniel's response took even my dad by surprise: "Yeah, but Dad, it's not *my* money, right? It's *God's* money. Isn't that what you taught us?" So Daniel, at sixteen years old, wrote a $10,000 check to help a community of people he'd never met. And he did it because that's the model our parents had set for him throughout his entire life. The crazy thing is, it wasn't difficult for Daniel to give that money. He saw a need and he had the money to help, so he gave it. The beauty of that story is that Daniel learned the value of giving as a little boy, so when he turned sixteen and had real money in the bank, his opportunity—and his desire—to give was magnified. That can happen when a child grows up in a family that values giving.

Dave: Insert extremely proud father right here. Watching Daniel make that decision at only sixteen was unbelievably satisfying as a parent, but I think God was smiling even more, because He started working on a selfish young guy named Dave at about the same age. Grace could be God changing me enough that it then changed my family tree. If I could go from extreme self-centeredness to watching one of my children give that much, that freely, then anyone can. And anyone includes you.

GIVING TIME AND TALENTS

Rachel: I think people often get confused about what giving really is. Like Dad said earlier, giving is rooted in stewardship. We're supposed to be good managers of *everything* that God has given us, and that includes more than our money. It's so easy for families to fall into the trap of giving a percentage of their money without ever stepping outside their comfort zone and really giving of *themselves* in the world. That's why I teach families the "Time, Talents, and Treasure" idea of giving. In addition to giving our treasure (money), we should freely give from *all* of our resources, especially our time and talents.

Popping the Bubble

The many comforts and conveniences in our culture make it easy for kids to grow up today in a kind of bubble. Having a warm, dry bed and three good meals a day seems like a given. Walking through the house and throwing your iPod, cell phone, and laptop into your backpack on the way out the door becomes routine. And hopping into one of the two or three cars parked in the garage to drive to school feels more like an annoyance than a blessing. If we're not careful, all of these wonderful things can pile up around us and keep us from seeing the world outside the safety of our comfort zones.

Mom and Dad popped that bubble every chance they had. As Dad's business grew and became more successful, they got even more intentional about making sure we always kept our blessings in perspective. They knew the danger of raising kids in a wealthy home totally removed from the heartache and hard life that so many people experience on a daily basis. My parents were committed to not raising three spoiled brats who knew how to handle money but never looked for ways to bless other people. And so they forced us out of the safety of our home and into "the real world" fairly often, always giving us creative intentional opportunities to give of our time and talents.

My Time and Talents, Their Money

When I was fourteen, my friends and I spent a lot of time at the mall. Pretty much every Saturday, Mom dropped two or three of my friends and me at the entrance to the mall, and we'd spend hours and hours walking around. We didn't really have money to spend every week, so I'm honestly not sure what we even did all day. But it was still one of my favorite things to do—wandering around all the stores with my friends, talking, laughing, and getting a ninety-nine-cent taco at the food court.

One Saturday morning, while I was probably already planning a trip to the mall, my mom approached Denise and me with an idea. Around that time, Mom and Dad had gotten involved with a local ministry organization that focused on young women who had come out of abusive situations or struggled with depression, addictions, or eating disorders. The focus of the ministry was to give these girls a safe place to heal. That Saturday morning, Mom said, "Today I want you two to go pick up a couple of young ladies at the ministry and take them shopping. I'm going to call ahead and ask the director there to choose two girls around your age who need some clothes. You can pick them up, and you all can go to the mall for the day."

Now, I'd like to say that I immediately thought this was a fantastic idea, but that wasn't what I thought at all. I actually felt really weird about it. I mean, these girls were going through some stuff that I couldn't even imagine. I didn't know what I'd say to them or what we'd talk about all day. I'm sure Denise and I made up some excuses as to why we couldn't do it, but Mom saw through it. After we whined a bit, Mom cut off the discussion. We were going, end of story. Mom gave us an envelope full of cash for the girls' clothes, and that was that. All I knew was that my Saturday was heading in a very different direction than I had planned.

A couple of hours later, Denise and I pulled up at the ministry and picked up the two girls. It was a little awkward at first, but by the time we got to the mall, we were all laughing and chatting like old friends. Denise and I realized pretty quickly that, despite the problems they were working to overcome, the girls were just like us. I remember walking through the mall, having a blast with our new friends. They were so nice, and they were so excited to go shopping! For Denise and me, going to the mall wasn't a big deal, but one of the girls told me that she hadn't been shopping—let alone to a mall—in two years. Two years! My little fourteen-year-old mind was blown.

The girls had so much fun trying on clothes and basically getting a wardrobe makeover. They hung out in the dressing rooms, and I would run around the store grabbing armfuls of clothes for them to try on. We had a nice lunch in the food court, and then it was time to go. We headed back to the car with what felt like a dozen shopping bags and two new friends.

When we got home, Mom greeted us at the door and asked us how it went. I was so excited that I couldn't stop talking. I went on and on about how much fun we had, how sweet and appreciative the girls were, and how cool it was to be able to share one of my favorite things (shopping) with two girls who never got to do it. Then Mom asked me a question that has stuck with me ever since. She said, "Rachel, did you have more fun *last weekend* with your friends or *today* shopping with these two girls?"

Without hesitation, I said, "Oh, Mom! Today, no question! We had so much fun!"

Mom smiled and said, "Yeah, it's fun to give, isn't it?"

It was . . . and still is. That afternoon made a big impact on me as a young girl. It was such a powerful example of a wise mother taking advantage of an opportunity to pair something she knew her daughters loved with a big need in the lives of two other girls. And we can't forget that the whole thing was possible because Mom and Dad had an envelope full of cash specifically marked for giving. Even though I was a teenager and didn't have a lot of my own money to give, my parents gave me the chance to use *their money* along with *my time and talents*. The result was an afternoon that blessed two young girls in need and changed my life—and my view of giving—forever. That's what happens when your kids learn *how to give* and *why to give*. They go from living in a world where everything is about them to realizing that there are other people in the world who need their help.

Creating Opportunities to Give

Dave: Sharon and I have always looked for opportunities that were part of everyday life to teach our children hands-on lessons about money. Sometimes, if the teachable moment did not occur naturally, we would manufacture a moment or an event. For instance, there were a couple of years we modeled giving by choosing an angel from the "Angel Tree," a program that provides Christmas presents for kids who have a parent in prison. As Sharon and I took our kids to find the perfect gift for our angel, sometimes the only results were three whiny kids who argued to buy something for themselves and two frustrated parents who worried about facing jail time if they killed one of their selfish offspring. Not exactly the intended spirit.

One year we volunteered to deliver the gifts bought by other families for the Angel Tree program. Taking the Ramsey kids on that ride and letting them see firsthand the children who, without this program and the generosity of others, would have had a very bleak and meager Christmas was mind-blowing for my kids. We called those "bubble-bursting moments"—when the "everyone-lives-as-good-as-you" bubble bursts. We regularly looked for bubble-bursting moments because they helped create grateful-ness in our children.

Another giving adventure my kids got to see in action was a "12 Days of Christmas" gift-giving campaign for a family that had lost their jobs and were too proud to ask for help. Some members of our church youth group asked our family to do the driving, and for twelve consecutive nights, we secretly put gifts, necessities, food, and even a Christmas tree on the family's front porch. To my knowledge, the family never found out who did it. Getting to sneak up and play Santa on a front porch was great fun for our kids.

The worst giving adventure we experienced was when I took one of my kids to deliver groceries to a family who had called our church asking for help. We went to the store and the church food pantry and bagged up what we thought were some great meals. When my preteen and I walked to the front of that house, we were feeling pretty proud of ourselves about helping someone in need. But when we set the groceries on the kitchen table, the woman became irate, saying she had asked for a certain kind of potato chips and a certain bag of candy. The lesson here is that giving isn't about getting the response you want. It's about the condition of your heart and spirit. Every situation won't go perfectly, but you can at least be caught trying.

AGE-APPROPRIATE GIVING

Rachel: Not long ago, I got into a conversation with a man at the airport while waiting on a flight. He asked what I did, and I told him I was on my way to speak to a group of parents about kids and money. He lit up and started telling me how he and his wife try to be intentional about training their kids how to handle money. The conversation shifted to giving, and he told me that he makes his children use their own money to buy birthday gifts for their friends whenever they go to a birthday party. I'm not sure I'd personally recommend that, but what he discovered by watching his kids was really interesting.

He said that the younger his kids were, the more generous they were. They would spend more money on a toy for a friend than they would spend on themselves. But as they grew older, he noticed a shift in how much they'd spend on others versus how much they'd spend on themselves. At some point as they grew up, the lines crossed and they became more interested in getting themselves something nice and less concerned about what they got their friends. I thought that was an interesting observation. At least in this one example, the kids were much more open and excited about giving when they were younger than they were when they got older. That won't be true 100 percent of the time in every family, but I do believe little kids have more of a free spirit when it comes to giving. Maybe they haven't yet learned to hold money tightly the way the world eventually warns them to do. So, when your children are young, encourage that spirit of giving and sharing. Do whatever you can to keep that childlike spirit alive!

Introducing the Give Envelope: Ages Six to Thirteen

We've already talked a lot about the Spend and Save envelopes for kids; now let's talk about the most important one: the Give envelope. In the Ramsey house, when we received our five-dollar commissions each week, Mom and Dad had us put at least one dollar in our Give envelope. That actually breaks down to 20 percent, but there's no real magic behind that number; it's just what worked well in our family, and it was easy math since we were paid in single dollar bills. You can decide the amount or percentage that works best for your family, but I'd suggest at least 10 percent of your child's money. That's a great baseline for giving as an adult, so it's best to get that into the kids' minds as early as possible.

When I went to church each Sunday as a little girl, I took my Give envelope. Around age six, I started putting my own dollar in the red velvet offering bag as it passed by. That was such a great experience for me. Too often, parents just give their child a dollar for the offering as they walk into church each week. When that happens, the child isn't really *giving* anything—he's just a little deliveryman for the *parents'* money. There's no emotional connection between working for the money and choosing to give it away.

The fact that Mom and Dad made me work for the money I put in the offering bag gave me the opportunity to learn how to truly give, and it made it so much easier for me to keep giving as I got older and my income increased. John D. Rockefeller once said, "I never would have been able to tithe the first million dollars I ever made if I had not tithed my first salary, which was $1.50 per week."

Now, as a working adult, I tithe every single paycheck and don't think twice about it. I understand, as I have since I was a little girl, that my income isn't really mine. There's a portion to be shared with others. That's the legacy of giving that my parents passed down to me.

Adding Service to Giving: Ages Fourteen and Up

As your kids become teenagers and have more independence, it's time to introduce the concept of giving of their time and talents, as well as their money. Encourage them to find ways they can serve by doing things they already enjoy and are good at. In the Ramsey house, all three kids were expected to participate in some kind of mission trip, and all three of us had life-changing, mind-blowing experiences as a result of these trips.

Remember how my parents always looked for ways to pop the safe little bubble we sometimes lived in? Well, there's no better way to pop the American middle-class bubble than to send your child on a mission trip to a struggling part of the world. Seeing other countries, other cultures, and how the people live— sometimes in extreme poverty—can permanently change your teenager's entire worldview.

Most of the time teens come back totally changed people. They may get to see a part of the world where people literally have nothing—often not even what we'd call necessities—yet they have a joy that is indescribable. Of course, you don't have to travel overseas to find that kind of poverty and need. If a global mission trip isn't in your family budget, you can still find plenty of opportunities for you and your child to serve here in the U.S. The goal is to make sure they see this as an opportunity to give their most valuable resource: their time.

CREATING LIFELONG GIVERS

Dave: When Rachel was in kindergarten, her teacher gave the students an assignment to draw a picture and write down what they would do if they had $100. I don't know how long it has been since you've had a kindergartener, but to a child that age, $100 might as well be $10 million. The teacher then copied and bound the pictures and captions into a small book. She sent the book home with the kids, and we noticed it as we were looking through Rachel's school papers from that week. Sharon and I sat on the floor in front of the couch reading the little book and laughing out loud. Those little kids sounded a lot like "grown-ups" today. Scott said if he had $100, he would buy a car that changes into everything. Allison was more realistic—she said she would buy a little dollhouse with her $100. Andrew, the budding terrorist of the class, said he would buy a football, a gun, and a bomb. (It was comforting that our child was in the same class with him.) Reid said he would buy a convertible. Kathy would buy a swimming pool with a whale like Willy from the movie *Free Willy*. Anna Kathryn would buy a house with a cat. (I guess with $100, she could at least get the cat.) Rachel was never our shy child. She was always doing something loud and outlandish, so we started to dread a little what her page might say.

When Sharon and I finally turned to Rachel's page, we were completely caught off guard. We looked at each other and realized we were both crying. Rachel's response was, "If I had $100, I would give it to the poor people." Maybe we were proud or being a little cheesy, but just four short years before this, we were in bankruptcy court, broke and broken. So to see one of our children understand that giving really matters gave us encouragement that, with God's help, we really could change our family tree. We really could raise children who not only got money but got great joy from giving it.

Catching your kids at outrageous giving, or even with a spirit of giving, is enough to bring any parent to his or her knees. But just like we didn't get it right every time, they won't either. The key is to praise them when you catch them in the selfless actions. Tell them the beauty of seeing God working in their hearts. And when they don't get it right, give them grace. Not every child is a natural giver, but the good news is that giving can be nurtured in them.

CHAPTER SIX

Budgeting
Tell It What to Do

Rachel: It was the hallway that went on forever. Finally I reached the door at the end of it, marked by a nameplate with the title "Executive Branch Manager." I took a deep breath and knocked on the door. I was fifteen years old, and I had a one-on-one appointment with the head of my local bank. It wasn't a social call. This was not going to be pretty.

The day before, when I came in from school, I found a letter from the bank on the kitchen counter. The envelope wasn't thick enough to be my normal bank statement, and it was rare for me to get mail from the bank, so I was curious as I opened it. When I read the opening lines, my heart skipped a beat. I discovered some new terms that day—phrases like *overdraft* and *insufficient funds*. The bank was writing to inform me that I had bounced three checks. That's right: *Dave Ramsey's daughter* bounced three checks. That's like the city's best dentist having a daughter whose teeth are rotting out of her head.

A little later, I heard the sound of the garage door opening. Dad was home. This could be bad. I had no idea what he was going to do. He came in and immediately read my face. The first thing he said was, "What's wrong?" Apparently, I'm not great at hiding my emotions. I walked across the kitchen, handed him the letter, and held my breath. *Here it comes*, I thought.

But it never came. He put the letter on the kitchen counter and looked me in the eye. I'm not sure what I was expecting, but I know it wasn't what he actually said. In a perfectly calm, not-mad-at-all voice, he said, "Okay, Rachel. First thing in the morning, you're going to call the bank and set up a meeting with the executive branch manager. Then you're going to go meet with him in person by yourself. And you're going to sit across from him and apologize for lying. You told him you had money in his bank to spend, but you didn't. That was a lie."

I was always a pretty respectful teenager, but I *am* my father's daughter, and sometimes my emotions get the best of me. I cocked my head sideways, put a hand on my hip, and asked, "Seriously? This can't be for real."

"Oh, yes, Rachel. I'm dead serious." The way he said it got the point across. I knew there was no use pushing it further.

The next morning, a Saturday, I called the bank and got a 9 a.m. appointment with the manager. I couldn't drive yet, so Mom dropped me off at the entrance. As I walked through the bank doors, it suddenly struck me that I had never been inside a bank by myself before. I didn't know who to talk to or where to go. I walked up to the teller behind the counter and asked if she was the branch manager. She laughed a little and said, "No, sweetie. His office is down the hall and to the right." So I started that long walk down the seemingly endless hallway.

When I found the branch manager's office, he introduced himself and offered me a seat. I sank into a huge leather chair and shifted nervously, my feet barely touching the ground. The manager flashed a smile and said, "Before we talk about whatever it is you want to talk about, I just want to tell you I'm a big fan of your dad. I think he's doing a wonderful thing, talking to millions of people on the radio every day about how to be responsible with money."

Ouch.

"Now, what can I do for you today?" he asked.

I looked across that enormous desk and said, "Well, sir, I'm here to apologize for lying to you."

"Excuse me?"

I handed him the letter I got from the bank and said, "Well . . . I, um . . . I told you I had money in your bank to spend, and I didn't, so three of my checks bounced. I'm here to ask for your forgiveness."

He stared at me for what seemed like forever, then said, "Ms. Ramsey, did your father put you up to this?"

I completely broke down. Tears poured down my face, and I said, "Yes! Isn't it *horrible*?"

More than a decade and several counseling sessions later (kidding), I can laugh about it. But you know what? I haven't bounced a single check since. Plus, the bank manager felt sorry for me and waived my overdraft fees! Dad set me up to learn a powerful lesson in an unforgettable way, and I'm so glad I learned it at fifteen instead of twenty-five.

Studies show that about one-third of banks' total revenue comes from fees; they're literally counting on people messing up their accounts.[1] Largely because of that painful meeting with the bank manager that Saturday morning, I'm not one of them. Although some may think that Dad's idea was an extreme way to make a point, that was the first and last time I ever got careless with my checking account and budget.

BUDGETING FOR YOUNGER KIDS

As we get into the budget discussion with kids, I need to set up one ground rule for you, the parent: You have to do a household budget every month. You can't teach your children to do something you aren't willing to do yourself. More is caught than taught, remember? With budgeting, that means your kids need to see you do a household budget and live by the principles you're teaching them. If you aren't already doing a budget or if you honestly don't know how, don't worry. We've got tons of tools, books, classes, and free budget forms to walk you through every detail. Check out daveramsey.com to get started.

Create Teachable Moments

Kids under fourteen don't really need to do a written budget. At this age, their envelope system *is* their budget. By teaching your children to work and divide their money among the Spend, Save, and Give envelopes, you're already teaching them the basic framework of budgeting. This doesn't need to go on paper, but I still recommend writing down their bigger saving goals like those we talked about in Chapter 4. This at least gets them used to the act of writing down goals as they work toward them.

Even though they aren't writing up their own budget forms every month, there are still some creative ways to get your younger kids involved in the activity of budgeting. A friend recently told me about her Saturday morning budget sessions. She and her husband do a monthly budget together, and because she is the nerd of the family, she gets it back out every Saturday morning to catch up on her online banking and double-check everything against the budget. So practically every Saturday morning, her four-year-old daughter, Abby, finds her at the kitchen table with her laptop, budget forms, cash envelopes, and a calculator. Abby knows exactly what her mom is doing too. She runs to her playroom, grabs her Dora the Explorer toy cash register, and sets it up on the kitchen table beside her mom's computer.

Abby will sit with her mom for maybe ten minutes, asking questions about money and offering her the plastic nickels from her toy cash drawer. "This is for the budget," she'll say. Abby's mom will show her daughter the long list of things they have to do with their money each month. No, she doesn't sit her four-year-old down and make her fill out a preschool budget form, but my friend is intentional about sharing that experience with her daughter. Think about that: Abby will go her entire life seeing a monthly budget as a perfectly normal, healthy thing to do. Even at four years old, it would be weird for Abby to come downstairs on a Saturday morning and *not* see her parents working on the family budget.

Get Your Kids Involved

Dave: The oldest child is often the one the parents experiment on. So as Denise, our oldest, grew from a small child to a preteen, we realized our teaching of money skills had to grow up with her.

One evening I was sitting at the kitchen table writing checks for that month's bills. Denise was probably a little under ten years old at the time, and I heard this tiny chipmunk voice ask, "Whatcha doin', Daddy?" I hate to admit it, but I was in accounting mode so I did not see it as a sweet moment. I just saw a kid with great potential to bother me. But when I turned and looked at her face, I saw someone interested in her daddy and the grown-up mystery he was working on. And it occurred to me that it was a teachable moment. I suddenly had the bright idea to teach her how to fill out a check. I remembered learning how to fill out checks in my lawn-cutting business as a young boy, and I thought it would be a great lesson for Denise. She climbed up in a chair beside me and, propping herself up on her knees, began writing out checks as I instructed her.

Then the unexpected happened. She filled out the check for the electric bill and wrote in $238 and stopped. She looked at me as if a light bulb had come on over her head, astonished that electricity could cost so much. Then I let her know that amount was for only one month. "So that's why Mom is always on us to close the door when we go outside to play," she said.

Wow! Not only did Denise learn how to fill out checks that night, but she also surprised me by recognizing value. She became my bookkeeper there for a while. Eventually her attentions moved elsewhere, but I will never forget that experience. And of course, I've often wondered what the clerk at the electric company must have thought when she opened our envelope and saw the check with a third grader's printing on the "Pay-to-the-Order-of" line.

Teach Budgeting by Example

Rachel: One day when I was about seven years old, I went grocery shopping with my mom. The cashier rang everything up, and I watched Mom pull two $100 bills out of the white Food envelope she always kept in her purse. I looked up at her with a shocked expression on my face and said, "Mom! It costs *$200* to buy groceries for us?"

She looked down and said, "That's right, Rachel. And when your brother gets a little older, it's going to cost a *whole lot more!*" So even as a little girl, I was able to start making the connection between working, budgeting, and spending money on necessities like food. That powerful example only happened because I had parents who lived on a budget and a mom who took the time to show me how it all worked.

Your children will also learn the language of budgeting by simply listening to the conversations in your house. I can't tell you how many times I heard my parents say the phrase "It's not in the budget!" when I was young. Sometimes *budget* felt like a cussword to us kids, but that phrase taught us something important: A budget creates boundaries. That's the great thing about being purposeful in how you plan your money—it sets limitations for you.

When you implement those limitations in your family, your kids will learn a powerful word. It's a word that has practically been removed from our culture today. A word that has no place in the realm of political correctness. A word that many parents today are too scared to use with their kids. The word is NO. That word is such a precious gift to children, even if they don't realize it. Let them hear you say no, not just for stuff *they* want, but also for stuff *you* want. "No, we can't afford it." "No, it's not in the budget." "No, I don't need that today." Young kids usually won't see the value in the word, but I promise, it will make an impression. They'll start to learn financial boundaries, whether they know it or not.

BUDGETING FOR TEENS

Whenever I talk to a group of high school students about budgeting, I always get the same response: "Do a budget? Are you kidding me? I don't have any money!"

And I always say the same thing: "Yes, you do! Some of you have part-time jobs, and some of you get money from your parents. So you *do* have money coming in every month. Now you need to be intentional about where it goes." If you and your teenager are talking for the first time about how to handle money, there might be some confusion about how they should budget. Some parents pay for everything their teen does, and some parents make their teens pay for a majority of their expenses. Neither is right or wrong, but there are a few guidelines to go by when it comes to your teen and his budget.

Be Intentional

Dave: Remember, whether you are fourteen or fifty-four, a budget represents intentional living. In his book *The 7 Habits of Highly Effective People*, Stephen Covey says the first habit of people who win is that they are proactive. People who win learn to *happen to* things rather than to *react* when things happen. Proactive people are forward-thinking people, mature people, so they are seldom victims of circumstances. Teaching children to budget is simply teaching them to plan. John Maxwell says, "A budget is telling your money where to go instead of wondering where it went." Zig Ziglar used to say, "If you aim at nothing, you will hit it every time." If your three- or thirteen-year-old child looks at you with a confused expression when you ask where her money went, you know that she was not intentional or proactive and she did not have a plan.

Learning to look forward and plan is a skill set that will translate into every area of your children's lives: Planning out the writing of a term paper so they are not up all night the night before. Planning what classes to take in college to ensure they graduate in four years. A young gentleman planning an evening with his girlfriend and communicating that plan to her father when he picks her up at her front door. These are impressive kids you are growing. Children who can learn to plan and be forward-thinking are more poised and confident because life is not always happening to them—they are happening to life.

The Five Foundations

Rachel: Younger kids have simple spending, saving, and giving goals. That's why the Spend-Save-Give envelope system works so well for kids. But as your child hits her teen years, things start to get more complicated. To keep your teenager focused on the right priorities, we've come up with five specific steps to help her take control of her money and look toward the future. We call these The Five Foundations:

THE FIVE FOUNDATIONS

1. Save a $500 emergency fund.
2. Get out of debt.
3. Pay cash for a car.
4. Pay cash for college.
5. Build wealth and give.

The first foundation is all about emergencies, as we discussed in Chapter 4.

We recommend teens put $500 in the bank just for emergencies. Go back and review that part of Chapter 4 if you need a reminder on what an "emergency" might look like for a teenager.

The second foundation is crucial for long-term success: Get out of debt. We'll talk about debt in the next chapter, but for now, let me clear it up for you: Debt is owing *anything* to *anyone* for *any reason*. That includes car loans, credit cards, and yes, even student loans. Your child needs to know as early as possible that debt in any form will wreck his future financial success.

The third and fourth foundations deal with paying cash (and avoiding debt) on the two biggest expenses a teen and young adult will likely face: buying a car and paying for college.

The fifth and final foundation is the most important and usually the most fun: Build wealth and give. For teens, this mainly means preparing for future wealth building. If your child is busy saving up for a car and preparing to go to college, then he may not have money left to invest in a Roth IRA. That doesn't mean you shouldn't start the conversations, though. Remember, my dad spent time with me explaining how a mutual fund works. That was back when I was in high school, years before I ever invested a dime of my own money. Those conversations gave me a mindset of investing early on, so when I started my first real job out of college, I knew exactly what to do.

The value of The Five Foundations is that they teach teens how to prioritize their budgets. They lay out a sensible goal-based plan that comes alongside their monthly budgets and shows them where they're heading. Most of the students I talk to don't know where they're heading. They're wandering through their teen years, letting every dollar they have slip through their fingers. Worse, they're losing the best opportunity of their lives to learn how to handle money, save themselves a world of trouble, and set themselves up for incredible success.

Open a Checking Account

By age fourteen, it's time for your child to graduate out of the Spend-Save-Give envelopes and into a real checking account. That may sound scary, but it's an important step. Keeping up with a checking account as a teenager can teach them so many lessons. They'll learn how to interact with a bank, check their account online, actually reconcile their account, write checks (yes, they still need to know how to do this), and take responsibility for their money in a more adult manner. Sure, they may make some mistakes along the way (just like I did), but this is the best time in their lives for them to make those mistakes because you're still there to catch them when they fall.

Here's what my parents did for me, and it's what I suggest for you if you are financially able: Think about all the money you spend on your teenager each month. This includes things like clothes, club and sports fees, lunch money, and even car insurance if your child does not pay for that himself. If you're doing a regular, monthly household budget, you should already know what expenses are coming up for your child. But instead of simply paying for all those things yourself or giving him a check for each one individually, I want you to add up the total of all those things coming up for the next month, deposit that one lump sum into your teen's bank account, and then let *him* pay for each of those things out of the account. That means managing the money—doing a budget and making sure the money does

exactly what it's supposed to do—becomes your teen's responsibility, not yours.

Coach Your Kids

Dave: I agree that budgeting and managing money should be the
teen's responsibility, but your role is to watch over your children's
shoulders until they prove competency. You do not simply open a
checking account, throw money in it, and hope for the best. You
would no more do that than toss them the keys to a car, having
never seen them drive. Watch them, teach them, and gradually
back away as they prove they can handle the account and you see
that their decision-making skills are developing.

Balancing their checkbooks (reconciling the account) once
a month, every month, was a mandatory chore for each of our
teens. I looked over their shoulders to ensure that the account was
reconciled. This gave me the opportunity to see every transaction (I could also view these online during the month if I wanted),
and it gave me the opportunity to coach them on doing a better
job managing the account. Were all the deposits and debit card
transactions recorded? Did they know how to connect online
for easy reconciliation? We never even showed our teens how to
check their balances throughout the month. They didn't need to
because they kept track of their transactions, so they knew what
their balances should be.

It is your job as the parent to teach, coach, and make sure your
child knows how to handle a checking account *before* she leaves
home. All three of our children have attended four years of college
living on what we budgeted monthly. We almost never had emergency calls for money from our college-aged kids. Why? Because
they managed their own accounts under our wing all through high

school, and when they went away to college, they were already better at planning for expenses, budgeting their money, and balancing checkbooks than 98 percent of American adults.

Provide a Safe Place to Fail

Rachel: Sometimes when I explain the checking account method to parents, I watch their jaws drop as they say something like, "You want me to do *what?* But if I put all that money directly into their account and they can do whatever they want with it, they'll blow all my money!" This is a scary idea, I know. But just think about it: Your child *is going* to be responsible for his or her own bank account *someday*. What's scarier: you teaching them to do it now under your supervision, or them learning it on their own? They are going to have free reign to make all kinds of really, really stupid decisions and huge mistakes! But here's the good news: They'll get to do it in the safety of your home and under your protection. This is truly the safest time in your child's life to learn how to master a checking account. Trusting them with your money now may seem a little risky, but it's nowhere near as risky as sending them out into the world with no clue how to manage an account with hundreds of dollars in it. Dad always told us that if we were going to fall, he wanted us to do it while he was still there to catch us. That's a great plan, parents. Besides, we're not just giving them a big pile of money with no instructions, right? We're going to teach them how to do their own budget.

The Dangers of Debit Cards

Dave: I am from the check generation. We wrote checks at grocery and department stores, and we paid the electricity and water bills with checks. Now most of us pay our utilities and other bills online. In fact, our culture today uses debit cards for purchases more than both checks and credit cards combined. When our kids opened their own checking accounts and became responsible for managing their spending, I was horrified that they never wrote checks; 99 percent of their transactions were using debit cards. I wanted them to learn to write checks, and they did. But the methods in the marketplace had shifted, and I soon accepted that the debit card was the new way of life.

Whether your teen uses checks or debit cards, the key is to make sure they emotionally feel the money. Talk with them regularly to emphasize that this is *real* money, not just digits in an account. When teens do not handle actual cash, there is a huge danger of out-of-control spending because money doesn't feel real to them. It's just like another video or computer game. But debit card transactions take place with *real* money, so when you see spending that is over the top, step in and course-correct. Remind your teen of the emotional danger adults face as well when using debit cards or credit cards, and how not using real cash often causes them to overspend.

On Paper, On Purpose

Rachel: Whether he uses debit cards, checks, cash, or online payments, home base for your child's money will be the monthly budget. We recommend the same kind of budget for teens that we do for adults: the zero-based budget. That means you want to spend every single dollar on paper, on purpose, before the month begins. That's the best, most effective way to budget at any age. When your income minus your expenses equals zero, you know for sure that you've accounted for every single dollar. If you leave any money sitting in the account without actually assigning it to a category in your budget, it *will* disappear. A budget should tell your money *what to do*.

Having the budget discussion with a teenager can be a challenge. Trust me, I've heard all the excuses. "But Rachel, I'm in high school. My entire net worth consists of a half-empty Starbucks cup and an iTunes gift card I got for my birthday!" I get that. But if your teen has a part-time job or actually works like we teach, and you're putting money in her bank account for her own monthly expenses, then she's going to have a *big pile* of money to manage. That means she must actually budget that money, just like you and I budget our paychecks. Getting into the habit at this age reinforces the fact that budgeting teaches boundaries.

The simplest starting point is a basic paper budget. For years, Mom and Dad ran our entire household budget on nothing more than a yellow legal pad. You can get a lot more sophisticated than that if you want to, but the truth is, a piece of paper is really all you need. We even provide a basic Student Budget form in the back of this book to help you and your teen get started. Whether you use our form, software, online tools, mobile apps, or even a legal pad, the process is pretty simple.

At the start of the month, your teen should add up all the money she will earn or receive that month. This includes income from work outside the home, the commissions she still may earn for chores, the money you add to her account for her basic expenses, and money she receives from any other source. Add all that up and write the total at the top of the page. That's your child's income. That number represents the total amount of money your teen will have available to spend that month, so make sure it's correct.

Then she will write down every single thing she knows she'll want to spend money on that month. We're talking *everything* here, from clothes to club fees to gas for her car. If she plans to see a movie with her friends, it should be on the paper. If her best friend has a birthday coming up and she knows she'll buy a present, it should be on the paper. Help your teen think of everything she plans to spend; if it's not on the paper, it's not in the budget! It's also smart to have a miscellaneous category for things that pop up unexpectedly, expenses she may not have been able to plan for.

It's worth noting that we always put "Giving" and "Saving" at the top of every one of our budget forms. God owns it all, remember? That means giving should be the first thing we do with our money. After that, your second priority is to pay *yourself*, so saving money goes next in the budget. If those two categories are not at the top of the budget, many teens—and yes, even adults—say, "I can't give or save because when I get to the end of the budget, there isn't enough money left!" I simply show them that their budget is upside down.

Dave: The beauty of teaching children to plan their giving and saving is that it actually causes them to give and save. We never give or save until that becomes a bigger priority than the worries of the day. And giving and saving almost never become a priority until they become part of our plan to win with money. Few people give large amounts of money on impulse. Few people save every month in their Roth IRA on impulse. These are acts of maturity. Adults devise plans and follow them; children do what feels good. As a parent, I tried to raise my children to be adults, not children in oversized bodies. So as they aged, Sharon and I progressively entrusted them with more and more adult-like responsibilities, ones that demanded maturity.

Rachel: Once your teen has written down all her expenses, it's time to do the math. Subtract all the expenses from the income. If the expenses are more than the income, then she's spending more money on paper than she has coming in. Help her go back and adjust the categories by trimming the budget a bit. If there's money left over, then she needs to go back and add to a category or double-check The Five Foundations. She can put the money toward whichever step she's on. If her emergency fund isn't up to $500, then she can build that up. Or if she is ready to save for a car, the money could go in her car fund. The goal is to get that number at the bottom of the page to zero. That means every dollar is accounted for *on paper, on purpose.*

Dave: Keep in mind that you are trying to get a fourteen- or fifteen-year-old to engage in an adult activity. Some days getting them to dress themselves is a challenge. As you push through this, remember that you are applying continuous pressure on them to do a budget monthly. This is not a one-time meeting and then they've got it. They are teenagers, which means you may sometimes seriously consider murder versus coaching. Drama, drama, drama. You cannot discuss abstinence one time and expect them to stay out of the backseat of some car. This is ongoing, and you may not know if you got through until they are twenty-five years old and they wake up and realize you were not as mean or crazy as they thought. I was twenty-four before my parents became intelligent again. Persevere. Keep pushing. Sometimes you'll feel like you are talking to a thirty-four-year-old and sometimes you'll think you are talking to a four-year-old. But don't quit.

Budgeting for Upcoming Expenses

Rachel: The monthly zero-based budget is one part of your teen's financial plan, but we're not quite done yet. Now we need to see how to plan for big expenses that are coming up a few months down the road. Say it's March and your teen is already thinking about Christmas presents for her friends. Or maybe it's January and she's already dreaming about that perfect prom dress. We call those things "upcoming expenses," and they have a place on the monthly budget too. Check the back of this book for our Upcoming Expenses form to help plan for those events.

Here's how it works: Have her write down the item (prom dress, spring break trip, etc.) and how much it will cost. Then she'll write down how many months she has to save up for it. Divide how much she needs by how many months she has, and that shows your teen how much she'll need to save every month toward that goal. That monthly chunk should go into her monthly budget so she'll have the money on hand when the time comes. If it will take more than a couple of months to reach the goal, then I suggest putting that money in a separate savings account. You want it safely away from the regular monthly spending money so she doesn't accidentally spend her spring break money in January. I'm not saying she needs a separate account for every savings goal, though. A single savings account for all of the individual upcoming expenses will work fine.

Doing a monthly budget and planning for upcoming expenses are definitely important steps, but let's not go overboard. I think it's a great idea to get your teens used to budgeting, but don't beat them over the head with their budget every month. Give them some freedom to make their own mistakes. Be careful to make this a positive experience for them so they can grow to love the process and benefits. If you stand over them and require monthly budget checks and mid-month budget audits, they could hit college and go into a "budget rebellion" that derails their whole plan. Remember that fine line between grace and legalism? It definitely applies to how you guide them in budgeting. But here's the wonderful thing: If they can learn how to live on a budget at fifteen, then they'll be ready to take on the world at twenty-five. There will be a confidence and dignity there that far too many young adults just don't have.

THE WEDDING BUDGET

Even if you do the world's best job teaching your child how to budget from age five through twenty-five, and even if your kid is great at writing out detailed budgets and tracking every expense, there's still one big event looming out there that will really test how seriously you and your family take this whole budgeting thing. There's one gigantic, life-changing party that's probably sitting out there in your future, especially if you have a daughter. There's a single day that can literally make or break years of budget training in your family. And guess what? It will also be the most emotionally charged time of your family's life. Break out the checkbook, because it's time to talk about paying for a wedding.

My Big Day
It should be no surprise to you that when the Ramsey girls got married, there was no blank-check, whatever-you-want-sweetie,

the-sky's-the-limit kind of attitude from my parents. They were so excited, and they loved my future husband, Winston, but Mom and Dad were obviously going to be realistic when it came to the wedding expenses.

Winston and I dated for a year and a half before he popped the question. From the first day of our engagement, we started planning my . . . er, I mean *our* . . . dream wedding. Oh, who am I kidding? I had been planning my wedding for most of my life! I actually dressed up as a bride for Halloween when I was four years old. I watched *Father of the Bride* so many times that I already knew what I wanted my wedding to look, sound, and feel like. Yes, I had enough maturity to realize that the wedding is just *one day* while the marriage is for *life*, but still—I was ecstatic. My wedding was going to be beautiful!

Mom and Dad took us out to dinner soon after Winston and I got engaged so we could all have the wedding budget talk. Mine was the first wedding in the family, so it was new territory for all of us. Because they trusted me with money and knew I had a lifetime of experience managing it responsibly, Mom and Dad decided to give me one final, enormous teaching opportunity: They let Winston and me run the entire wedding budget ourselves. They told us at dinner how much they would give us toward the wedding, and they actually gave us one check in that amount. As an extra incentive, they told us that we could keep any money we had left over after the wedding. I vividly remember Dad saying over and over, "Rachel and Winston, this is it. This is all the money we are going to give you. When the money's gone, it's gone." Is this sounding at all familiar?

That week, we opened up a checking account under both our names for the wedding budget, deposited the check, and got to work. Winston and I still kept our separate checking accounts for everything else, though. Managing the wedding budget together was a great exercise, but it's never a good idea for a couple to actually mix their incomes and regular accounts until they are officially married. It's sad, but things can still go wrong during an engagement. I've talked to ex-fiancées whose would-be spouses went crazy and destroyed the other's finances as they were leaving the relationship. Don't let your child get caught in that disaster. Of course, if Mom and Dad had concerns about Winston and me getting married, they wouldn't have given us the wedding money at all!

Over the next several months, everything went great. We ordered the flowers, booked the reception location, and I found the perfect wedding dress. Two months before the big day, there was only one item left on the list: chairs for the reception. I was getting ready to place that order when I stopped to check our wedding bank account balance. My heart sank. There wasn't enough money in the account! I went into full Rachel-drama mode, complete with tears and some mild hyperventilation. My roommate said, "Rachel, calm down! Just call your parents and ask for a little more money." I cried, "You don't understand! They *won't* give me any more!"

I pulled myself together enough to call my wedding planner. We did what many couples today would find shocking: We started cutting things out of the wedding plan. The flowers in the sanctuary turned into berries and holly (which actually looked great for our December wedding). We decorated *every other* pew for the service instead of dressing up every one. We canceled the car service from the church to the reception. We cut every corner I could think of, but there still wasn't enough left to get the chairs we needed for the reception. I was stuck.

Dave: She "needed" those chairs. Ha, ha, ha.

Rachel: Finally, torn between competing emotions of embarrassment and humility, I called home. I told Mom and Dad what happened and how hard I had worked to fix the problem, but I was still short. They told me that they'd discuss it and call me back. I can only imagine that Mom spent the next hour convincing Dad to help me out, because when they called back, they agreed to give me enough to cover the chairs. Dad was pretty clear with me, though. He said, "Rachel, this is the first, last, and only time we're giving you extra money." I was actually surprised, but I shouldn't have been. My parents knew I had done everything possible to fix the problem, and they knew that I wasn't running around spending money on all kinds of crazy things. We'd been having those discussions my whole life, so we knew we could trust each other. In their final budgeting lesson to me before I left their home for good, my parents chose to live out my favorite money principle: Too many rules is legalistic, but too much grace is enabling. I'm so grateful for parents who were able—and willing—to keep that balance with me throughout my life.

If a daughter's dream wedding is in your future, I want to make a few specific suggestions on how to handle it. Remember, this is going to be an extremely emotional time for all of you, so it's best to make these decisions now while you still have a little perspective on things—before the emotion of realizing your little girl is getting married takes over!

Set a Firm Budget . . . and Stick to It

Put a specific, realistic number in place for the wedding budget. Do not try to wing it. If you do, you'll get home from the wedding, add up all the receipts, and choke on your leftover wedding cake. CNN reports that the average wedding in the United States costs a whopping $28,000, but even that figure doesn't include *every-thing*.[2] When you add up the most common expenses, the actual figure starts to look more like $33,000–35,000, and that doesn't even include the engagement ring, rehearsal dinner, or honeymoon. All these things add up quickly, so you should always know the upper limit of what you have (or are willing) to spend before you start. In budgeting terms, that's basically what you'd put on the income blank, and all the items underneath are expenses.

Pay Cash for the Engagement Ring—A Note to Guys

Dave: When Sharon and I got engaged, I made payments on her .29-carat diamond engagement ring. I was proud and didn't think twice about financing. Now, thirty years later, that ring is a keepsake in our safe, and she has a much larger and nicer diamond that I paid cash for.

Don't do what I did all those years ago. Save and pay cash for the engagement ring. Make sure the ring you put on her finger is hers. Know your budget and only buy what you can afford. There is absolutely no correlation between the size of a ring and the success of the marriage.

How Much Should You Spend?

Since the average household income in America is around $52,000 and the average wedding is around $28,000, I think a good guideline is to never spend *more* than half your annual income on a wedding. So a family that makes $80,000 and spends $65,000 on their daughter's wedding is silly and out of control.

If the rule is to spend no more than half, then spending way less than half is even better. Most of us know at least one couple who has been married for fifty years and got married on the preacher's back porch with rings from a bubblegum machine. I have attended many weddings that were wonderful, creative, and cost less than $10,000. I really don't care what the amount is for you. The most important thing is to have a limit and a plan—otherwise your sweet daughter might turn into Bridezilla and try to set a spending tone that can only be rivaled by Congress.

A Wedding Is Not an Emergency

If you have daughters, you might as well start saving for a wedding. Some families have a college fund and a wedding fund. This event is not a surprise, and it should not catch you off guard. The fact that our girls played "dream wedding" every other day when they were little was a good reminder for us to save and be ready. They both had beautiful weddings and married wonderful men, so it did have a bit of a fairytale ending.

Give the Couple Their First Budgeting Team Assignment

Rachel: I think Mom and Dad gave Winston and me a huge gift when they handed us a check for the wedding—and I'm not talking merely about the money. Even though Winston and I both knew how to budget, we had never worked together on one before. Managing the wedding budget and checking account gave us experience working as a budgeting team for the first time, and that was priceless. I'm blessed that we had a great experience, but I also know plenty of future brides and grooms who would be shocked at what they would learn about their potential spouse if they went through this process. It's great to talk about budgeting and money management in theory while you're dating, but actually seeing how your future spouse makes real decisions with real money may be a rude awakening.

If you're able to give your child her wedding money in one lump sum like my parents did, I definitely recommend it. The value goes far beyond the dollars. In giving the young couple that budgeting experience, you are giving them a huge head start.

Their Wedding Is Not Your Responsibility

Dave: Let's say you are reading this and you have a daughter who's engaged, but you simply can't afford to pay for a wedding. The purpose of this section is not to make you feel guilty because you can't write a big check for a dream wedding. You can only do what you can do. Regardless, you can lovingly guide your child by not going into debt for a one-day party, having a detailed plan, and coming up with creative ways to make the day happen. For example, we have some friends who asked a local farmer for flowers from her flower garden. The farmer was thrilled to help and made a generous donation of flowers, *tons* of fresh flowers. I have never seen so many flowers, and they were all free. Don't let guilt lead you into stupid decisions and a pile of debt; just do what you can to help make it happen within your family's budget.

Use Budget Ratios

Rachel: No matter where the money comes from—her parents, his parents, or no parents—the couple absolutely has to plan a budget around whatever amount they have to spend. Debt is not an option. Nobody wants to still be paying for their wedding cake on their fifth anniversary! That means everyone participating in paying for the event (bride, groom, *and* parents) needs to sit down and look at the total wedding budget. And when I say "budget" here, I'm not just talking about how much your child can spend; I'm talking about how much they have to spend *in each specific area*. I suggest breaking the total budget into categories and applying a ratio for each area.

As I worked on my wedding with my wedding planner, we kept some budget ratios in mind. But these aren't hard numbers. You should set your own ratios based on what's important to you. These are simply what Winston and I used.

Reception: I recommend budgeting 55 percent of your money for the reception, which is by far the most expensive part of the wedding. This includes the facilities, food and drinks, decorations, wedding cake, band or DJ, parking, and transportation.

Ceremony: I suggest spending 12 percent in this category, which includes the flowers for the ceremony (like the bride's bouquet), location, and officiant. Many people go crazy spending money here, but it's actually one of the easiest areas where you can cut expenses. When I had to cut costs out of my own wedding, this is where I started. I still had a beautiful ceremony, but I was able to trim some expenses out of my original plans just by tweaking my flowers and other church decorations.

Photography: Plan on spending 10 percent of the budget on the photographer and videographer. You could save a lot of money by having a friend take the pictures, but I honestly don't recommend it unless your friend is a professional. Wedding pictures will last a lifetime! You don't have to go crazy here, but make sure you are getting quality pictures. Interview several photographers. This is one area where you'll see a big price difference between professionals.

Wedding Planner: I recommend 10 percent for a good wedding planner. This is another area you could cut if you're on a tight budget, but if you can afford it, I definitely recommend getting a quality planner. This is someone who eats, sleeps, and breathes wedding details, and she does it without all the emotion that a bride brings to the table. Having someone else manage all the details is a huge blessing.

Dress and Tux: This is another area where many, many brides go nuts, but I recommend spending no more than 8 percent of the wedding budget on the dress and tux. Yes, I know there's the dream of "the perfect dress," but I personally believe the perfect dress is the one that makes the bride feel beautiful *without* breaking the bank.

Miscellaneous: Go ahead and plan 5 percent of the budget for the random, fall-through-the-cracks things that are a part of every wedding. These expenses might include bridesmaid and groomsman gifts, wedding bands, invitations, and thank-you notes. Be sure to include the marriage license!

In all of these areas, please keep in mind that these are *recommended* percentages. If the couple cares a lot more about one area than another, then weight the percentages in that direction. For example, one of my friends was adamant about a particular (expensive) dress that she wanted, so she rearranged her budget around that dress. Another friend put a high priority on the quality of the food, so she spent more than recommended on that. The truth is: we don't care *how* you divide the wedding money; we just want you to do it on purpose. If you raise one area, you have to bring another area down. If you go nuts and overspend in one area, that means you have less to spend in the other areas, so you'll need to rebalance your ratios. These ratios will be a blessing whether you have a huge wedding budget or are trying to get it done on the inexpensive side.

PLANNING MATTERS

Dave: Hidden in the bones of this chapter is the fact that you are teaching your child to grow into an adult—a *mature* adult who plans, budgets, is proactive, and does *not* act like a perpetual victim, waiting on someone else to fix her life. Budgeting nurtures maturity, which is necessary in so many areas of your child's life. So start with that three-year-old and teach her that a few weeks of budgeted saving will equal a toy purchase. Then progressively become more sophisticated in your teaching until you have a college student who can manage her own bank account and, eventually, her wedding budget. And if you follow the principles in this chapter, the great news is you will not only raise money-smart kids, but you will also grow responsible, money-smart adults who are poised, confident, and who won't be moving back into your basement when they are thirty-two.

CHAPTER SEVEN

Debt

It IS a Four-Letter Word

Rachel: *Well, this is interesting*, I thought as the little piece of plastic sat there on the restaurant table. It was November of my sophomore year in college, and I was out on a date with a guy I had been hoping would ask me out. I had seen him around campus and we had many friends in common, so you could say that I had developed a bit of a distant crush on him for more than a year. When he finally asked me out to dinner, I was ecstatic! He picked me up, and of course we both had the first-date nerves and anxiety, but the night went great. We talked all through dinner and really hit it off. Then the bill came. Now, I wasn't some crazy money girl who made everyone around me follow my no-debt rules. I did, however, like to watch how other people handled their money, so I was interested in what he'd pull out of his wallet. Call it "professional curiosity." That's when the guy I'd had a crush on for over a year pulled out his Capital One credit card, complete with a picture of an eagle soaring across it. I half expected Dad to burst through the doors from the kitchen with his giant pair of card-chopping scissors!

I thought, *Oh man, this will be interesting if this relationship goes the distance.* And sure enough, it did. That guy is now my husband, and looking back, we crack up about the fact that he paid for most of our dates in the first six months of our relationship with that Capital One soaring-eagle credit card. Obviously, once we got serious and marriage entered the discussion, we got on the same page about money. And no, I didn't twist his arm to get rid of that card; he let that eagle soar off all on his own.

DEFINING DEBT

Our culture is confused about debt, so let me clear up the definition for you: Debt is owing *anything* to *anyone* for *any reason.* Credit cards? Debt. Car loans? Debt. Mortgage? Debt. Student loans? Debt.

Prepare for the Lies

I don't know anyone who would come right out and say, "I absolutely *love* debt! I'm so glad I owe tens of thousands of dollars to the bank! I'm so blessed!" No, that'd be crazy. But what about:

"I'll always have a car payment."

"Of course you need a mortgage to buy a house."

"Student loans are 'good' debt."

I guarantee your child will hear these common lies all the time, and they'll probably start hearing them sooner than you think.

Your kids are growing up in the most indebted generation in history. The average college graduate leaves school with $35,000 in total debt—and that's before he ever gets a job![1] The great news for you is that you can prepare your child to avoid this financial mess. We've said it before: Winning with money is only 20 percent head knowledge; it's 80 percent *behavior*. If you still have kids living at home, then you are in the perfect position to teach them the behaviors that will keep them out of debt and set them up to win for life.

The Biggest Debt Myths

Dave: Normal in America is broke. So if you do normal behaviors, you will be broke, and if your kids are financially normal, they will be broke. In my book *The Total Money Makeover*, we cover a myriad of myths that normal people believe about debt. The financial industry has so successfully normalized debt through their marketing that most people don't believe debt-free living is possible.

But this book isn't for normal people. It's for people who have figured out that normal isn't good enough. This book is for *weird* people—people who are willing to act differently in order to become wealthy. And wealth is so unusual and abnormal that we must say it is weird. So if your goal is to take mediocrity to the grave and raise children who perpetuate your stupidity, then this book isn't for you.

When you realize that normal isn't working, you begin to examine the mythology believed and spread by normal people. Normal people say things such as: "You will never live the good life if you don't finance that thing you want but can't afford." Normal people also say, "You must build your credit." "You will always have a car payment." "You can't be a student without a student loan." And, of course, "You will always have a mortgage." This is the lingo, the language of normal people—people who live paycheck to paycheck and stress to stress, and who struggle all through life. Not me. As for me and my house, we have declared war on normal. We want total money weirdness!

Look Better Than You Are

Rachel: When I was in high school, I had a friend who drove a brand-new car, always had a new designer bag, and kept up with the latest fashion trends. When a group of us planned to go to a concert, though, she told us that she couldn't go because she couldn't afford it. I was shocked. I went home and told my parents how confused I was. Everything about her screamed wealth and success, but she couldn't afford a $150 concert ticket? I didn't get it.

Mom said, "Rachel, just because someone looks like they have a lot of stuff doesn't mean they actually own it. This may or may not be your friend's situation, but remember, debt makes people *look* a lot better off than they really are." That was such a powerful lesson for me, because in our household, debt was never an option. Even though I knew *about* debt, it didn't click until that moment that debt basically enables people to live a lie. They can look like someone they aren't. Debt allows you to put on a persona that everything is perfect, even though you may be broke, hurting, and miserable on the inside.

Dave: Texans have a phrase for this: "Big hat, no cattle." This means you are trying to look like something you aren't, and this façade will keep you in the poorhouse. In the story above, Sharon used the opportunity as a teachable moment. She addressed the problem of debt and drove the point home for Rachel.

Slave to the Lender

I discovered this idea of debt-free living through the lens of my faith. When we hit bottom, I began studying the Bible and found that it had pretty clear principles for handling money. The easiest, yet hardest, principle I found was debt is never a good thing. The Bible never calls debt a sin, and it is not a salvation issue. But nowhere in Scripture is debt mentioned in a positive light. Instead, it says, "The rich rule over the poor, and the borrower is slave to the lender" (Proverbs 22:7 NIV). *Slave* is a powerful word. A slave can't go where he wants to go or do what he wants to do because he has a master calling the shots. Why do you think they call it *Master*Card? The Bible says over and over that if you purposely put yourself in debt, you are a fool, you are a slave, and debt is a curse. There is not a single verse in the Bible that says something good about debt. So I have concluded that biblically speaking, debt is stupid.

If you are not a person of faith, then biblical truth may not matter to you, and that is your choice. But for me, as an evangelical Christian, I believe the Bible is God's Word and the Truth when nothing else is. From that perspective, once I learned that debt isn't biblical, it made *not* borrowing money an easy decision—it was an act of faith. It was also an easy decision because, having just been bankrupted, no one was lining up to loan me money, nor was I excited about getting back into the mess I had just gotten out of. At the same time, not borrowing money was the hardest decision I have made, because the financial community thinks I am nuts and sets out every day to tell me how primitive, unsophisticated, and backward I am for no longer believing the mythology that has guaranteed their financial mediocrity.

Preventative Medicine

Rachel: As we walk through some of the big misconceptions about debt, I want to remind you of something. I said earlier that I like to view my dad as the emergency surgeon, but I'm the preventative medicine. That's exactly what we're doing here: preventative medicine. So far in this book, we've worked to lay the groundwork for your child to win with money. If she does what we teach, she will win. It's a proven system that we've seen work more than a million times. But we can't just stop at what she should *do*; we also need to focus on what she should *avoid*. And the number one thing to avoid is debt. That includes credit cards, car loans, and yes, even student loans. If your child can stay away from debt for life, she can completely avoid most of the financial nightmares that this generation is facing, and she will never experience the stress of owing anything to anyone. That's what preventative medicine is all about.

THE BIG LIE: YOU NEED TO BUILD YOUR CREDIT SCORE

Dave: I get so frustrated with parents who teach their children that the credit score, or FICO, is their provider. Well-intentioned parents spend an amazing amount of time indoctrinating their kids with the lies of the system, the greatest of which is that you must "build your credit." The lie of normal says you must borrow money to build your credit so you can borrow money to build your credit so that you can borrow money. I wonder if that dog will ever catch his tail? My FICO score is zero, undeterminable. So how do I survive? I pay for things or I don't buy them. Weird, isn't it? Teach your children to be countercultural in a culture that has lost its mind.

Check our website or FICO's website. The algorithm that is used to produce your FICO score contains just a few mathematical items: 35 percent is based on your debt payment history, 30 percent on your debt levels, 15 percent on length of debt, 10 percent on new debt, and 10 percent on type of debt. Show this to your young teenager. Point out that 100 percent of your FICO score is based on debt, not on wealth. Zero percent is based on cash position or savings. Zero percent is based on income. Zero percent is based on net worth. Zero percent is based on investments or retirement savings. Zero percent is based on paying your utilities on time, buying food for your family, or living on a budget. Zero percent is based on financial discipline represented by saving up and paying cash for a car, college, a wedding, or even a house. One hundred percent of your FICO score is based on how often you say, "I love debt"—on how often you play kissy-face with a bank. A high FICO score does *not* say you are winning with money; it says you are successful at borrowing money. Normal people worship the great FICO; wealthy people don't. Teach this so loudly, clearly, and often to your children that when someone tries to convince them that they need to build their credit or credit score, they will look at that person with pity and relish their own weirdness.

Have "The Talk" with Your Kids

Rachel: One day back in my freshman economics class, the professor started going on and on about how important the credit score is. He told us that we couldn't buy a house or drive a nice car without a credit score. He said we had to protect that score at all costs. Then he leaned in and told a roomful of eighteen-year-olds that we all needed to go out, get a credit card, and begin using it immediately so we could start building our credit.

This may surprise you, but my parents and I never talked much about the credit score when I was growing up. We focused on things like work, saving up to buy things, paying cash, and why debt in general is such a nightmare. So when I got this advice from my college professor, I was confused. I went back to the dorm and researched it online, then I called Dad to ask him about it. He explained it to me, and in about five minutes he showed me how stupid that little number is and how it really has nothing to do with being successful or building wealth. When your kids get to college, they're going to get money advice from other people—even their professors. It may be good or bad advice, but either way, it's coming. Go ahead and prepare your kids by arming them with knowledge like my dad shared with me.

CREDIT CARDS

The credit card is one of the best ways to guarantee your child will live in bondage to debt his entire life. With every swipe, the banks will steal more and more of his future. The problem is, our culture has made credit cards the norm. People really believe you must have a credit card and that you just can't live life without one. And the debt that people walk into in the name of airline miles, cash back, and other perks blows my mind. So if I go $10,000 into debt with this credit card, I'll earn enough miles to buy a $500 airplane ticket? Uh . . . am I missing something?

The Credit Card IS an Emergency

Dave: Think about it: When is the dumbest time to go into debt? When you are broke. When you are in financial trouble and have no money, that's the worst possible time to borrow money, especially on a credit card with a high interest rate. It is ridiculous. Yet I have done it and you may have too. Why? Because no one ever trained us—like you are now training your children—to have a plan, to save, and to have actual money in an emergency fund. By now, your children should be seeing the fruit of the earlier chapters as it plays out in practical results, like not needing a credit card for emergencies.

"But I Pay Mine Off Every Month"

Rachel: One of the biggest problems I have with credit cards is the "I pay it off every month" mentality. I get that this is true for a lot of people (not for everyone who claims it), but even so, this is a terrible way to go through life. Using a credit card for daily expenses in the name of "convenience" is another way of saying, "I don't want to do a budget." I have never met someone who uses a credit card for everyday purchases *and* does a zero-based budget at the beginning of every month. Instead, the people who charge everything just pay the bill at the *end* of the month or, even worse, sometimes the *following* month. When you do this, you are throwing your income behind you, paying off things you have already used or done. That's like driving a car by looking only in the rearview mirror. You can only see where you've been; you have no idea where you're going or what it's going to take to get there.

After one of our live seminar events, I talked with a guy who had recently cut up his credit cards. He said, "Rachel, I used my Discover card for everything. If I bought it, I put it on the Discover because I wanted the cash-back bonus. But I had no idea what I was spending! On payday, I'd just send Discover most of my paycheck to cover the past two weeks of spending. Even though I was at least breaking even every month, I wasn't going anywhere. I didn't have any kind of financial future because I was too busy sending all my money into the past."

If you teach your kids how and why to budget, and if you teach them to avoid debt like the plague, they'll never see the need for a credit card. They won't need the "convenience," because they'll have an actual plan for their money. You want convenience? Teach your kids how to budget. If you want them in an endless cycle of debt their whole lives, go ahead and give them a credit card. It's pretty much that simple.

Cash Hurts

Dave: When your kids enter their teen years, they will be bombarded by credit card offers. By the time they are seniors in high school, they will be getting dozens of offers to sign up for credit cards. So when your child is in his early teens, lay a card on the table with fifty ten-dollar bills ($500) next to it. Ask your child which one feels like the *most* money and which one feels like *real* money. You want your teen to verbalize that cash has much more emotional weight than plastic. The danger of plastic not having the emotional weight of real money is that people spend more when using plastic than when using cash. Why? Because spending cash *hurts*. Handing a salesperson $1,000 in cash for a new sofa feels a lot different than flipping a piece of plastic up on the counter. Since personal finance is 80 percent behavior, train your child to *feel* money. They have to be emotionally impacted when making a purchase, or they will continually overspend.

Kids and Credit Cards

Rachel: Love them or hate them, you at least have to recognize what an amazing job the credit card industry has done in marketing their products to us. They figured out that parents have just about all the cards they can fit in their wallets, so the banks had to change tactics. That's when they started using something called "kiddie branding." If you stop to think about it, it seems ridiculous that Visa would spend millions of dollars marketing its product to little kids. But have you seen the Game of Life recently? It has the Visa brand all over it. That fits in perfectly with their "Life takes Visa" marketing message, doesn't it?

Monopoly has also gotten into that game and is offering a credit card version. When I was a little girl, I even saw a Barbie with a MasterCard attached to her tiny plastic hand—and a full-sized card for the child to play with. Why do the banks spend money putting their logo in front of an eight-year-old? Because ten years later, when that kid gets three credit card offers in the mail on the first day of college, she'll already know which one she wants. She'll subconsciously think, *Barbie uses MasterCard, so I should too.* You've got to teach your children to recognize these messages whenever you watch a show together or pick out a toy. Don't let a credit card sneak past you! Be on guard with your kids.

Credit Cards Don't Teach Responsibility

Dave: Sometimes parents will actually tell me that they are getting their teen a credit card to teach them to be responsible. Are you kidding me? Credit cards don't teach responsibility. They teach that you can buy something you can't afford today, but hope to pay for tomorrow. When you teach a child to lean on a plastic crutch, you are teaching them that they don't have to delay pleasure, or sacrifice, or save up and pay cash for things. You are teaching them that they don't need to save for a rainy day, because the plastic umbrella is always there. You are teaching them really bad values that will lead them into debt, which may take them a decade to clean up.

Cards Go to College

Rachel: One night back in college, a few friends and I took a study break and went to a local burrito restaurant for dinner. As we walked up to the place, we noticed a guy slightly older than us sitting at a table at the entrance. The table had tons of brochures scattered everywhere and a big banner overhead. He said, "Hey, girls, do you all want a free dinner tonight?" For a handful of broke college students, the answer was not difficult. As you can imagine, we enthusiastically said yes!

"Great!" he replied. "Just sign up for this credit card, and we'll pay for your dinner." I laughed it off, but one of my friends walked up and filled out the form right then and there. It took her all of about two minutes, and she was done.

After we got our food and sat down, I asked my friend why she did that. She said, "Oh, Rachel, it's no big deal. When it comes in the mail, I'll probably just cut it up. And if I end up keeping it, I'll use it just for emergencies." That phrase sent off alarm bells in my head. My parents had always taught me that's how so many people end up with a pile of credit card debt. They think they'll just use credit cards for emergencies, but then life happens and they end up in debt, one little "emergency" at a time.

That's exactly what happened to my friend. A month after getting that card in the mail, her laptop broke, so she ran out and charged a brand-new one on her "emergency" credit card. Soon after, a mutual friend got engaged, and she charged a bridesmaid dress too. The next month, she received a $1,100 credit card bill in the mail. She didn't have the money to pay it, which created a lot of stress. She had no idea how to pay the bill, and she panicked just thinking about what would happen if her parents found out. Within a month, my friend went from carefree to full-blown panic mode because of that little piece of plastic. And it was all for a $7 burrito.

Too many college students see getting their own credit card as a rite of passage into adulthood. But getting a credit card doesn't make your student an adult; it makes her a slave to debt and sets her on a potentially lifelong course of spending money she doesn't have. When you train your child from a young age how to spot those marketing tactics, and if you teach her that the borrower truly is slave to the lender, you'll empower her to walk right past the debt salesman at the college burrito restaurant.

Debit or Credit?

Dave: The only plastic we use in the Ramsey house and the only plastic we taught our kids to use is the debit card. Since a debit card is attached to a checking account, your teen has to have money in the account, or they will trigger insufficient funds charges. Remember, Rachel knows this all too well. Take the time to teach your child that while the debit card looks like a credit card, it is a much more responsible way to make purchases, and it won't get them into trouble unless they use it incorrectly.

CARS

The answer to almost every radio call I get from people struggling with debt is, "Sell the car." I can't tell you how many calls I've answered that start with someone saying, "Dave, we've got a $50,000 household income, and we owe $52,000 on two cars. What should we do?" Um, hello? *Sell the cars!* This isn't rocket science; it's simple math. You will never get out of debt or build wealth if you have a car payment. And, whether you want to believe it or not, a $500 paid-for car *will* get you to work and back home again.

When we lost everything, I was driving a beautiful Jaguar. I loved that car, but I had to let it go, and I refused to go into debt again for a car. So a friend graciously offered to let me borrow a car—an old Cadillac that's primary color was Bond-O. The Bond-O Buggy was so ugly that calling it "hillbilly" would have been a compliment. But I drove that car until I could pay cash for a nicer one. Hopefully you won't have to drive something quite as ugly, but you may have to lower your standards a bit until you can afford to pay cash.

Let your kids see you make sacrifices on cars to keep from borrowing money. And if you are currently making payments on a car, for Pete's sake, pay the thing off or sell it! I'm not just interested in your kids winning; I want you to win too!

The New Car Smells . . . Like Depreciation

If you have established that your teen will save up and pay cash for his first car, then he won't have to worry about considering a brand-new car because he simply won't have the money. Remember, though, that we never miss a teachable moment. While looking at used cars, make sure you swing by the new car lot and show your teen what the new version of that car costs. When he sees a $23,000 price tag on the new car and a $7,000 price tag on the used version, the lesson is immediate—the value of new cars drops like a rock in just a few years. This gives you the opportunity to teach your child that cars are not investments. They are the largest purchase "normal" people make, and they drop in value the second you drive them off the lot. Cars do more financial damage to middle-class Americans than almost any other financial decision. Paying cash for a car and buying a used one is the shortest path to building wealth.

"I'll Always Have a Car Payment"

Rachel: I often hear adults say, "I'll *always* have a car payment." What they don't realize is that this is not only affecting their lives, but also the lives of their children. I cannot stress enough how important it is *not* to have your children believe this lie. One of the best ways you can show your kids that they can live life without a car payment is to involve them in buying their first car. Mom and Dad used 401DAVE, which was great because it showed us that we could save up and drive a car we actually paid for. If you don't have this conversation with your kids, there's a good chance they will grow up to believe that they'll "always have a car payment." That's a scary situation, and I'll tell you why.

The average car payment in America today is right around $492. This is a lifetime plan for many people, and they never stop to think about what those car payments cost them in the long run. When you run the numbers out over an adult's working lifetime, you really see how this whole mindset is costing the average American literally millions of dollars.

Let's say your child has bought into the lie of, "I'll always have a car payment." He makes it out of college and gets his first real job. Now, since he's bought into the great American myth about cars, he probably also feels like he *deserves* a new car. That's what many people do when they get a new job, right? That's true at twenty-five or fifty-five. They celebrate a $400-a-month raise with a $500-a-month car payment. So at twenty-five, your child goes to the car lot, signs up for a ridiculous car loan, and starts a long forty-year journey into car payment purgatory. He drives away with the average car payment of $492 a month for sixty-three months.

What do you think forty years of car payments will cost him? Let's do the math. In this example, your child at age twenty-five just signed up for a car loan with a $492 monthly payment. If he learned early on to save up and pay cash for cars, and if he learned about budgeting, debt, contentment, and the other things we're talking about in this book, he wouldn't have that payment. That means he'd have $492 extra in his monthly budget to save and invest. If he were to invest that $492 into a good growth stock mutual fund his entire working lifetime—age twenty-five to sixty-five—he would retire with $5,846,153! He'd be a million-aire by age fifty-one and have almost $6 million at retirement simply because he paid *himself* a car payment all those years. That's incredible! I don't think you should let your kids out of the house until they fully understand this. This one decision can literally change their entire lives.

Don't Tell Them—Show Them

Okay, I need to do a little tough love here. You have to talk to your child about this. More than that, you need to show him that you're serious about it by avoiding car debt yourself. If Mom and Dad had made me work and save for my own car at sixteen, but then they ran out a week later and bought a new luxury car on payments, the only thing I'd remember is that my parents put me through a worthless exercise that they didn't really believe in. More is caught than taught, remember?

BUY A HOUSE, NOT A MORTGAGE

A reasonable mortgage is the only type of debt that Dad and I won't get too frustrated with you about. But that doesn't mean you must have a mortgage to have a house. What if you taught your child to have a crazy, extreme goal when it comes to buying a house? And by crazy and extreme, I mean what if you showed him how he can pay *cash* for a house someday? You may think I'm nuts, but I've seen this happen over and over, and it's always amazing.

The House That Cash Built

My friend Christy grew up in a loving family, but they always struggled with money. At their lowest point, they actually had to skip dinner because they couldn't afford to eat. Even as a little kid, Christy was determined to never face those kinds of struggles as an adult. That meant debt would never be an option for her. No credit cards, no car loans, and . . . drumroll, please . . . no mortgage. Ever. But with big plans for a family and a nice house, that meant she had to do things differently than the rest of the world.

In her teens, she started saving money—*lots* of money. She took care of her Five Foundations, but she always kept the dream of a debt-free house in front of her. She was blessed with an awesome husband who felt exactly the same way about debt, so they combined their resources and kept plugging away at the goal. When they finally started looking for a house, their real estate agent tried to get them to use their savings as a down payment on a bigger house, but they wouldn't have that. They just answered, "No, let's start this conversation over. *This* is how much money we have to spend, and this is *all* we're going to spend. We don't 'deserve' a bigger house just because we can get a loan. We have *this much*, so *this* is how much house we 'deserve.'"

So, at twenty-eight years old, this amazing couple sat down at the closing table with a cashier's check and bought their beautiful four-bedroom home outright, with no lender anywhere in sight. Can you even *imagine* what kind of wealth this couple can build throughout their lives just because of their commitment to live totally, completely debt free? It's incredible! I want your kids to have that kind of life too.

Start the Conversation

Christy and her husband prove my point: It *is* possible to live a completely debt-free life. Don't let anyone tell you or your child that you "need" a mortgage to own a home. You don't. Sure, it's hard and it takes a long time, but your child has all the time in the world. You just need to point him in the right direction. So I recommend starting the debt-free-house conversation with your child when he's a teenager. This doesn't mean he needs to start a house fund at fourteen; remember, the big savings goals for teens are paying cash for a car and college. While he works on those goals, though, you *can* talk to him often about how to save long term and how amazing it would be to write a check for a whole house someday. And if he gets out of college and has a lot of money left over in his college account because of scholarships, then he'll already have a head start on a house fund. Sure, this is a big goal, but it's not impossible. It just takes time and focus.

Renting (for a While) Isn't a Waste

Some people think that you have to buy a house the minute you get married or graduate from college. That's crazy! There is absolutely nothing wrong with renting for a few years. It's a terrible long-term plan; you don't want to rent forever. But renting for a little while when you're just starting out—or while you're saving up a lot of cash to buy later—is a great idea. Talk to your teen about this, because as soon as she gets married or gets her first real job, people will crawl out of the woodwork saying, "When are you going to buy a house? You need a house! You're throwing your money away with rent!" No, she's not.

Renting for a season shows patience and wisdom. Too many people wreck their lives with ridiculous mortgages simply because they rushed into buying a house way before they were ready. And by "ready," I mean they are completely out of debt, have a full emergency fund of three to six months of expenses in the bank, and have a down payment of *at least* 10 percent (but 20 percent is better). Until your child is at that point, buying a house shouldn't even be on her radar. Buying a house is a privilege still in her future, so show her how she can one day do it with cash.

But if They MUST Take Out a Mortgage . . .

Dave: Have I mentioned I hate debt? If you call my radio show asking my advice on borrowing money, I guarantee I will mess with you. Debt is the biggest thief of your financial future. I don't even like mortgages. Nevertheless, the one debt I don't yell at people about (but would still rather they not have it) is a home mortgage. I don't borrow money, but if you are going to take out a mortgage, buy super conservatively so you can pay it off quickly, and teach your kids to do the same. Our rule of thumb is never take a mortgage where the payment is more than 25 percent of your take-home pay with a fixed-rate, fifteen-year mortgage.

CHANGING GENERATIONS TO COME

Rachel: Cars, credit cards, and looming mortgage mistakes can be scary, but I'm afraid there's something even more frightening that is creeping up on this generation: student loans. The student loan debt in this country is completely out of control. Total student loan debt has even overtaken total American credit card debt. It's definitely crippling an entire generation of young adults before they even get their first real job. It's a big deal, and we'll talk about how to avoid that trap in the next chapter.

But before we leave the debt topic, I want to give you some encouragement. If you as the parent have these conversations with your kids and show them how to live a debt-free life, you have given them a tremendous gift. Most parents today don't think to talk to their kids about debt, and some have even bought into the debt lie so much that they teach their kids to believe it too. That's how families stay in debt generation after generation. But you can choose a different path, one that your children will thank you for for the rest of their lives. That's my story, remember? I am so grateful for parents who showed me how to live debt free, and now I get to reap the benefits of that knowledge by putting it into practice in my own adult life.

Dave: What if you took pride in your family name and what it meant as a financial legacy? After we went broke, Sharon and I decided there were certain things a Ramsey does not do (at least our little branch of the tree). A Ramsey does not borrow money. Really. If you are starting with small children and you have time to become debt free, let me propose a truly family tree–changing idea. Declare early and often to your family that "The (insert your last name here) Family" does not borrow money. You may think this is simply a nice sentiment, but it is much more than mere sentiment; it is a mathematical possibility, even a probability. If you are debt-free, live with savings, and do a zero-based budget each month, could you not save for your child's wedding and college? Of course you could and would. But let's get radical. Let's say your home is paid for in our plan, so you have tons of cash flow. What if you not only saved to pay for a wedding and college, but you also decided to pay cash for your child's first house?

"Well, Dave, wouldn't that give them a mentality of entitlement?" I hear you asking.

No. You have raised them with the principles Rachel and I have discussed in this book. They have a heart of gratitude, they have a work ethic, and they are on autopilot for saving and budgeting. If that is the child you have raised, give them a paid-for house. A friend of mine has done that for two grateful, productive children, and he only asked that they sign a one-page letter of agreement. That little letter says that in return for a paid-for house, they agree to never borrow money for anything ever, and they agree to save and give paid-for homes to their children. Generation after generation of this man's family will live in financial peace. His kids, grandkids, and hopefully everyone else in his family tree will never make payments again. This great gift took two things: money— the intentional building of wealth—and the intentional training of money-smart kids. The payoff is an incredible legacy.

CHAPTER EIGHT

College
Don't Graduate from I.O.U.

Rachel: "That's really what we want to do with our lives, Rachel. But we just can't do it. Our student loan payments won't allow it."

That was the end of one of the saddest discussions I've ever had after an event. I'd just spoken to a group of about 3,000 college students at a private university, and a senior from the audience came up afterward to talk. He was engaged and planned to marry his fiancée that summer. He and his future wife had a heart for serving other people, and they both felt called to mission work overseas. As he told me about his fiancée and their passion for missions, I could tell he was really excited—for a minute.

He then sadly told me he had used student loans to pay his tuition all through school, and he'd be graduating with $80,000 in debt. Leaving college with a four-year degree and $80,000 in the hole seems like a nightmare for anyone, but especially for someone with aspirations for a less-than-lucrative career like foreign missions. And it got worse. He said that his fiancée *also* owed $80,000 in student loans. I could hardly believe it. That meant this amazing young couple with a heart for serving other people was about to start their married life together with $160,000 in debt—just in student loans. As you can guess, the math didn't work for them to give their lives away serving others. They *couldn't* give their lives away because someone else already owned them: Sallie Mae.

This may seem like an extreme example, but I've seen the same thing happen over and over again to lesser degrees, like with a friend of mine who was recently offered her dream job. She was so excited to actually get a job doing what she loved, until she started crunching the numbers and looking at her budget. The starting salary the company offered wasn't enough to cover all her bills—which included tens of thousands of dollars in student loans. In the end, she had to turn down the job and take a slightly higher-paying job that she wasn't nearly as happy about just to make her payments. That's a really sad situation, and it's something I want your child to avoid.

STUDENT LOANS: A ROADBLOCK TO THIS GENERATION

Student loans are a roadblock to this generation. Current college graduates are leaving school with an average student loan debt of $27,000—and obviously more for private, prestigious, or graduate schools.[1] Altogether, there is roughly $1 trillion in total outstanding student loan debt in the United States today, and student loans have recently surpassed credit cards in total debt owed.[2] Graduates will carry those loans around with them for years or even decades; they can't even escape them through bankruptcy because federally backed student loans are not eliminated in a bankruptcy. The short-term gain of student loans doesn't even compare to the long-term pain your student could end up with. There's no doubt: This is a generational crisis, and, as a parent, you need to be ready.

Student Loans Limit Options

In Chapter 7, we talked about Proverbs 22:7, which says, "The borrower is slave to the lender." I thought about that verse after meeting the graduating senior who had a passion for missions. He and his future wife will start their lives together with $160,000 in student loan debt. Before they do anything else—before they even get jobs, pay for the wedding, and find a place to live—they will start $160,000 in the hole. If you want to know what their lives will probably look like, all you have to do is look at the math.

Let's say that when this couple graduates, they each get a job paying $31,000 a year. After taxes, that's a take-home pay of around $2,000 a month each. Want to guess what the payment on $160,000 in student loans is? It's right at $1,800 a month—a little less than one spouse's total take-home pay. That means this guy and his wife will both have to work full time, forgetting their dream to serve as missionaries—and one of them will work forty hours a week *just to make the student loan payments.* That's it. They won't be able to save that money for a house. They won't be able to use it for vacation. They can't use it for new clothes or a night at the movies. One of them will basically work all day every day only to send almost their entire paycheck directly to the lender.

That means the other spouse will have to cover all the household expenses solo on a take-home pay of $2,000 a month. If you figure $900 rent on a one-bedroom apartment, $250 for utilities, and $550 for food, that leaves this couple with $300 a month for anything else they want or need to do like buying gas, maintaining a car, replacing old clothes, or even getting a haircut, not to mention things like saving, giving, or having a little fun now and then. This couple will be stuck for years and years of their lives, and it is all because of student loans that not only didn't help them achieve their dreams and passions but also actively prevented them from doing so.

Even though $160,000 in combined student loans is a lot higher than average (but $80,000 isn't *that* uncommon), the problem isn't much better for graduates with less debt. In a survey of recent graduates with school debt, 47 percent say they are putting off buying a house or car, 76 percent are putting off saving for the future, and 35 percent are putting off starting a family.[3] They are finally ready to graduate, but all the financial mistakes of the past four years have snuck up on them and robbed them of the joy of getting out of school and starting their lives as working adults. This situation breaks my heart.

Busting the College Debt Myth

As a culture, we have thrown up our hands and surrendered to a lie. College advisors, financial aid officers, high school counselors, students, and even parents have bought into the lie that you can't be a student without student loans. We hear that signing up for tens of thousands of dollars in debt is the only way to get through school.

But the great news is that there's hope. There is a way for

your child to get an excellent education without going into debt. It doesn't matter if your kid is heading to college next fall and you have nothing saved or if he's still in diapers and you have eighteen years to save. There are ways to get this done, but it's going to take some hard work—for both you and your student. The debt-free college plan isn't always easy, but it is definitely the best way in the long run. It all comes down to five things: parent planning, school choice, financial aid, working while in school, and your student living a reasonable lifestyle.

PLANNING AHEAD: THE PARENTS' ROLE

Dave: I have talked to hundreds, possibly thousands, of parents over the years about when and how they should contribute to their kids' college expenses. This is such an emotional issue for so many parents. I've talked to single moms who are working two jobs just to keep food on the table, but they're guilt-ridden because they aren't able to put money away in a college account. It's like there's an assumption that "good" parents pay for college or take out loans for their kids, period. This is ridiculous! Yes, there are some great ways to save for college, but college saving still has to make sense in your overall financial plan. Let's try to take some of the emotion out of the discussion and look at how you, as the parent, can help pay for your child's education.

When to Start Saving
If your kids are young and you've got a while before they graduate from high school, there are some great ways to save money for college. Yes, you need to be putting money aside for their education

every month as part of your budget, but there are some ground rules to remember. First, only start saving when you're financially ready. That means you're out of debt, you have a full emergency fund of three to six months of expenses, and you're contributing 15 percent of your income into retirement. *Only then* should you start putting money away for college.

I want to repeat that just in case I lost you: You have to start funding your retirement *before* you save for your kids' college. You can do both at the same time if you're able, but if it comes down to one or the other, you have to take care of your retirement. College may or may not happen for your child, but you will definitely retire one day. And when you do, you're going to need some money to take care of yourself. Your child will have plenty of ways to pay for college, but there's only one way for you to prepare for retirement, and that's to save money *today*. You're not a bad parent for taking care of your retirement first; you're actually being wise.

First: The Education Savings Account

The first $2,000 per year you save should be put in an ESA, an Education Savings Account. I recommend putting it into a good growth stock mutual fund. Your broker can set up the $166.66 to come out of your checking account monthly. If you start that account when your child is born and the mutual fund grows at 12 percent per year (about what the market has averaged), you, yourself, will have put in only $2,000 for eighteen years, totaling $36,000, but the account will have grown to about $126,000. The ESA is the Roth IRA of college savings in that it grows tax free, so the $90,000 of growth the account experienced in our example above has zero taxes, which will save about $30,000.

Second: The 529 Plan

The good 529 plans are simply the big brothers of the ESA. They also grow tax free, but you can put more into them. But remember, there are bad 529 plans. Stay away from plans that fix or control your investment options. You also need to stay away from the prepaid state tuition plans. With those, you are counting on the state to manage money well, and we all know how well the government handles money. Also, your return when you prepay for something is based only on the inflation rate of the item. So with tuition inflation averaging around 7 percent per year, that is all you will make on your money. If you are going to do a 529, then only do the kind you can put into a growth stock mutual fund and that allows you to control and move the investment.

But what if my child gets scholarships? Is my money trapped in a 529? No. Current law allows you to draw out an amount equal to the scholarship with no taxes or penalties. So you get the tax-free growth, and you didn't even spend the money on education.

Three Nevers

The ESA and 529 plans are great tools to save up and pay for college, and if you're able to put that into your monthly budget, then by all means do it! But there are three things you should *never* even consider when figuring out how to help your kids pay for school.

First, debt should never be an option. The first part of the chapter focused on all the trouble student loans are causing this generation, and we definitely want to avoid that. But we also don't want to put a whole generation of parents in debt because they decided to take out loans on behalf of their kids. Heading into retirement with $30,000 or more in brand-new debt will totally crack and scramble your nest egg. Your lifestyle and options at retirement will be limited, and you'll be the one carrying those student loans—possibly to your grave. Don't do it!

Second, never cosign a student loan for your child. If you do, you'll undo all the money training we've covered in this book. You'll show her that, when it comes down to it, you actually do believe debt is an option. Besides, cosigning a loan will change your relationship. You'll both be in debt together, and that puts a huge strain on the relationship. If she can't make the payments, you'll be responsible for them. Imagine Thanksgiving dinner if you're sitting there next to your child after making a year's worth of student loan payments because she couldn't (or wouldn't) pay. Imagine the resentment on your part. Imagine the guilt and shame—or worse, entitlement—on her part. Don't jeopardize your relationship with your child. Nothing is worth that price!

Third—and this is something I've seen so many parents do— never, *never* cash out your retirement accounts to pay for your child's college expenses. Dumb, dumb, dumb! Remember, your retirement is 100 percent up to you, but your kids have plenty of ways to pay for school that we will cover in the following pages.

Who Is Responsible for Paying for College?

Rachel: The ESA and 529 work great if your kids are young, you're out of debt and saving for retirement, and you have several years to save for college. But what if you have a high school senior and no idea how to pay for higher education? That's a tough situation, but it's not just a money problem; this is a huge emotional hurdle for a lot of parents. This comes down to a question of responsibility: Who is ultimately responsible for paying your child's college bills? Here's a hint: It's not you.

College is not an entitlement. Your child does not *deserve* to have his higher education paid for (completely or in part) by you. You have clothed him, fed him, and given him a safe place to live for eighteen years. If little Johnny wants to go to college and you're not in a position to help him, then he can do it on his own. He can go to school 100 percent debt free if he's willing to work for it. We're going to cover several ways for him to do that in this chapter, but debt will not be one of them.

Of course, I don't want you to surprise your teenager with this news on the night of his high school graduation. Tell him early in his teen years how much (if any) you plan to pay toward his college education. Talk to him about the different things he needs to do while in high school so he'll be ready with his portion. Remember, the two big savings goals for a teen in high school are paying cash for a car and paying cash for college. Saving up and paying for his own car is a huge lesson in hard work and independence; doing that for college really kicks everything up a notch because it gives him the chance to invest in his own future.

If you're able to pay part of the tuition, then get creative in how you share the tuition costs. I spoke with one student recently whose parents told her they could cover half the tuition costs. She worked all spring and summer to pay her fall tuition, and her parents paid the spring tuition each year. I thought that was a great way to work together, and it also gave the student some time each spring and summer to save up a pile of money for that fall's tuition. Knowing she had to come up with the tuition money every other semester kept her focused and working instead of sitting around wondering when her parents' money would run out.

The point I am making here is that, at age eighteen, your child is technically an adult and should take responsibility for her own life. That doesn't mean you shouldn't help if you can; I think it's a huge blessing to be able to pay for a child's education. But it does mean you shouldn't feel guilty if you can't pay. This is a crucial time in your child's life, and it's probably the first real opportunity you have to see what she's going to do with the financial lessons you've been teaching her up to this point.

CHOOSING A SCHOOL

Choosing a college or university might be the most critical part of graduating debt free. This one decision will shape so much of your child's future—and I'm not necessarily talking about what school's name is on the diploma. The biggest key is to choose a school that your child can afford. And by "afford," I mean the same thing I mean when I talk about affording a car or any other purchase. It means your kid can actually *pay* for it; it doesn't mean your child thinks she can afford the *monthly payments*. Too many students (and parents) lose sight of the fact that a college education is a major purchase, just like a car or a house. It's not a *right*; it's a *purchase*. So you need to treat it like a big purchase and shop around!

Dave: I am convinced that we don't have a student loan crisis in America as much as we have a parenting crisis. As my children grew into adults, it was easy to assume that because they were full-size humans, their decision-making skills and wisdom had kept up with their physical growth. We all know that isn't the case. As parents, we want our kids to act mature and make their own decisions, yet too many of us let them wander off into a minefield with no direction. If you hired an eighteen-year-old to work in a company you own, you would assume he had no training and no experience, and you'd never even consider letting him make major decisions on a $100,000–200,000 project by himself. If you were to do that, you would be a fool, and anyone looking in from the outside would assume the poor new kid is being set up for failure.

Yet this is exactly what parents do every day with their children when deciding what college they should attend and what field of study they should enter. We abandon our children to their best efforts, and our federal government will guarantee their debt even though they have no collateral, no experience, no wisdom, and generally no clue. Then we as a society stand back and say we have a student loan crisis. No! We have a parenting crisis and a foolish government. The result is a student loan debacle where a twenty-six-year-old racks up $120,000 in debt to get a master's degree in German Polka History, and he ends up working at a burger joint.

You must lovingly guide your "grown" teen in his college choice and field of study. Keep the lines of communication open, and be ready to pull the money away if necessary to save him from himself. Don't finance insanity and call that blessing your child.

A dad called my show one day distraught because his seventeen-year-old son had selected a college that was very expensive, and the dad could not figure out how he was going to pay for it. This father said to me, "What am I going to do? My son told me this is the school he is going to go to." Whoa! Who is running the household here? My response was that this was a parenting problem, because my seventeen-year-old doesn't tell me anything.

Don't Cross the State Line

Rachel: As my brother, sister, and I got older, Mom and Dad started having the college talk with us. My parents obviously live what they preach, so we were blessed that they were able to save up for all three of us to go to college. Dad told all of us early on that he and Mom would pay for our college, but it wouldn't be a blank check. He said we had to keep our grades up, graduate in four years (anything over that was up to us), and go to an in-state public university. Of course, as the semi-rebel child of the family, I told him I wanted to go to Auburn University instead of staying in Tennessee. He said, "Okay, you better start saving. Mom and I will still pay the in-state amount, but you have to cover the difference." As I started researching tuition amounts, you can imagine that my findings were a bit discouraging. Today the average cost of tuition and fees at an in-state public university is $8,655 per year. If you were to step over the state line and attend a public school in that state, the cost would almost triple to $21,706.[4] So I humbly went back to my parents and told them I would start applying to Tennessee schools. All three Ramsey kids went to a public state school, and we all stayed in Tennessee to do it.

Mom and Dad could have afforded to send us anywhere we wanted to go. But having the money to go anywhere didn't mean it was a good idea. Now, as an adult, I realize there is almost never a reason to justify spending three times as much to go to another state. When I travel and speak at colleges, it drives me crazy when a student tells me he took out student loans so he could get a degree that's exactly the same as what he could have gotten in his home state for a third of the cost. Not smart. I am glad my parents taught me the common-sense approach to choosing a college.

The only time it might make sense for your child to leave her home state for college is if she's going to a school in a neighboring state that has a reciprocity deal with yours. Reciprocity is an agreement between some states that reduces or waives the out-of-state premium for students in nearby states. For example, Minnesota has reciprocity agreements with Wisconsin, North Dakota, and South Dakota. That means students from those states could go to a Minnesota public college and pay at or around in-state tuition.

Private vs. State College

Dave: Your child can get an incredible education and have a wonderful college experience at a private school, but it comes at a price. The average cost of a private college is just under $30,000 *per year.* That's almost four times what he'd pay at an in-state public school. Is the education your child could get at a private school four times more valuable than what he'd get at a state school? Will a diploma from that small private school immediately make your future graduate four times more marketable when he hits the job market than a degree from a state university would?

Degree or Pedigree?

If you have unlimited funds or a free-ride scholarship, then by all means send your child wherever you want. I am not mad at private schools. There is a wonderful university in Nashville called Vanderbilt, a southern school with an Ivy League feel. Academically, it is a great school; however, tuition costs almost ten times more than the University of Tennessee, a public school. Is Vanderbilt better academically? Probably. Is it ten times better, and do their graduates earn ten times more? No. So to go deeply in debt for the pedigree to go with the degree is absolutely nuts.

There are hundreds of people on my team, and I have hired thousands of people for real jobs that pay real money since starting my company. To this day, I have never hired someone based on where he or she went to school. I have used lawyers to do work for me thousands of times in business, and I don't know where any of them went to law school. And I have never asked to see my doctor's diploma right before he started a procedure to confirm that his med school was a good one. It is mythology that a "good school" guarantees you'll earn more money or get more jobs. Sure, there are some jobs where people consider pedigree, but they are so few that you can't make your decisions based on that information. *The Wall Street Journal* recently published a study showing that more CEOs and board members of Fortune 500 companies graduated from state schools than from so-called prestigious universities.[5]

Again, I am not against private schools. I have a good friend whose daughter just got a full ride to Harvard. She should go! One of my family members got a full ride to Vanderbilt for undergraduate studies. He should go! Another friend who is a multimillionaire sent his daughter to his alma mater, a very expensive Christian university, and he paid cash. That is awesome! I have no beef with anyone attending these schools. But never let anyone, especially your own child, convince you that it is worth going $100,000–200,000 into debt just to get a pedigree.

Junior Pedigree: Private Elementary and High Schools

Many parents, including Sharon and me, have had to choose between sending their child to private versus public schools for elementary, middle, and high school. There are three major factors families consider in making this decision. One is safety. Parents may feel the public school their child is zoned for just isn't safe. The second factor is academics. Parents may believe a private school has superior academics to the public school. And then the

third factor is spiritual environment. For instance, a Christian—
Protestant or Catholic—may want their kids in a Christian school
for the spiritual environment that school offers.

Those are three really good reasons to consider a private school.
But to automatically assume that private schools are the only way
to raise your children well is absolutely absurd, and to assume that
your child will be more successful if he attends a private school is
ridiculous. There's just no credible research to prove this.

Growing up, although it was a different day, I attended public
schools. So when Sharon and I faced this decision for our kids, we
looked at the public schools in our particular county. There were
no issues with safety, and the schools had excellent academics.
And obviously the school system has to do things legally, so the
schools are not "Christian," but we are in the buckle of the Bible
Belt, so most of the teachers were Christians. Because we had the
best of all worlds, the Ramsey kids went to public schools.

As you begin to make your own decision, there are three things
you must remember. First, you cannot live in the land of drama or
fear. You can't overstate the safety issue to rationalize the purchase
—"Oh, my child is gonna die if I send him to that public school."
Don't overstate the safety issue as a parent.

Second, you can't depend on the school to be your children's
only model of a spiritual walk. Your children will not get this in a
Christian school if they are not getting it at home. It's your job to
lay the foundation for your kids' spiritual walks, not the school's
job. Anybody who's ever been around a "Christian school" knows
that a lot of bad things can go on there too. So to assume that it's
a bubble or a utopia is absolutely absurd.

Third, remember to use common sense when considering
academics. Are private schools sometimes academically superior?

Sure. But sometimes they're not. There is no correlation between attending a private preschool, elementary, or high school and future success. I see no evidence or research to support this.

Now, do private schools have higher graduation rates, do more of their students get into college, and are the schools academically superior? Possibly, but even then, we can't say that more private-school kids end up winning in life because of the schools they attended. A child's family environment, socioeconomic environment, neighborhood, and parents have a lot more to do with his future success than where he attends school.

So if you're going to look at private school as an option, it has to be a reasonable part of your budget. You cannot go into drama mode and bankrupt your family so your four-year-old can go to a private daycare. I talk to people all the time who are completely unreasonable about this. You must use common sense in the discussion and in making your decision.

Community and Online Colleges

Rachel: Local community colleges have gotten a bad rap. Sure, they may not be as exciting as moving into the dorm at the big state school, but there are enormous benefits in attending a good community college for a couple of years. Most degree programs focus on the same basic prerequisites for the first year or two—things like history, English, and foreign languages. If your student is on a tight budget, he could save a ton of money by knocking out those fundamentals at a community college. Most of these colleges work well with the nearby four-year state schools, so it's likely the course credits will transfer. He'll just want to check in advance to make sure every community college class he takes will transfer.

Let's say your child attends a community college for two

years and then moves to a state university for his final two years. If he graduates from the state school, that's the logo that will be on the diploma. You officially *graduate from* whatever school gives you the degree.

Dave: Online college classes are a great way for your child to get a head start while still in high school. Some universities will even let high school students attend free. Just avoid ultra-expensive online schools and most "online-only" schools, including a lot of the for-profit schools you see investing enormous amounts of money for television commercials. The best option at the most reasonable cost is to take online classes from a full-on, regular brick-and-mortar college.

Choosing a Major

Using a common-sense approach to picking a major is as important as choosing the right school. Your child should study something that interests her and that she is passionate about pursuing. But you are not to abandon an eighteen-year-old to her passions. A useless degree or field of study is just that—useless. So you have the duty of finding the balance between encouraging your child's passions, creativity, and dreams while simultaneously giving her the guardrails of common sense. If you err only on the side of practicality, you will guide—or force—her into something that is marketable but she hates. The paradox is she will never be successful because she has no passion. On the other hand, if you let her go unchecked into a major that is completely impractical, then she will also face disappointment. It is your duty as a parent to participate in the decision and to lovingly guide your child.

A twenty-nine-year-old man called my show recently with

a mess on his hands. He has a master's degree in opera, and he had racked up $120,000 in student loan debt to get the degree. To graduate with that degree, you have to be very, very talented— your voice literally becomes an instrument. His talents aside, he explained to me that he has never earned more than $35,000 in one year. Is a master's degree in opera a bad thing? Not at all! But where were his parents in this decision process? And how can a government allow a kid to borrow that much in student loan debt simply to end up making what he could have made with a high school diploma in another field? This is crazy.

NAVIGATING THE FINANCIAL AID MAZE

Rachel: There is a phrase you'll become intimately familiar with as soon as you and your child start exploring colleges. This phrase will either be a blessing or a curse depending on how you use it. Even though you'll see this phrase on documents, websites, and even office doors, no one really seems to understand what it means. This little phrase has enabled students to graduate 100 percent debt free, and it has caused people to graduate with more than $100,000 in student loan debt. As the parent, you need to get your head around all that it entails. I'm talking, of course, about *financial aid.*

Financial aid refers to all kinds of tuition assistance, from scholarships to loans and everything in between. It's a catchall phrase, and that's caused a lot of confusion for parents and students as they sit down and try to figure out how to pay for college. To get your kid out of college debt free, you both have to learn how to navigate through this maze.

Scholarships: Free Money!

The best, safest, most cost-effective way to pay for school is through scholarships. Shocking, I know. Scholarships really are free money, because you don't have to work for them, and you don't have to pay them back. Students can get awards for a million different reasons. Maybe you know your child well enough to realize that she's not the sharpest tool in the shed. That's okay. Sure, there are scholarships based on academic achievement, but there are just as many (or more) based on the most random criteria you can imagine. The harder you look, the stranger they get.

Think I'm exaggerating? I did a little research to see just how crazy some of these scholarships can be. I found one that's awarded to the student who creates the best prom dress out of duct tape. Another gives a cash award for showing off a milk mustache in public. I even found an actual scholarship that's given to the applicant with the best survival plan in case of a zombie apocalypse. I'm not kidding—these are *real* scholarships! Of course, having so many options means your student will have to work that much harder to track down and apply for as many individual scholarships as possible. This is where good old-fashioned hard work comes into the equation.

It's easy to blow off a $200 scholarship possibility because the amount looks so small. I hear that from high school students all the time. They ask, "What's $200 when you're facing a $10,000 tuition bill? It's just not worth applying for."

Wrong!

I always frame this objection a different way. I say something like, "Look, we're talking about $200 here, and all you have to do is fill out this application and write an essay. It'll take you about thirty minutes. If you get it, that means you earned $200 in half an hour. I don't know any part-time job that can touch that hourly wage!"

As your child hits her senior year of high school, I want to suggest a new part-time job for her: filling out scholarship applications. I recently talked to a new college graduate, and she told me that all through the spring semester of her senior year of high school, her mother made her fill out two scholarship applications every day. That took maybe an hour a day, and at the time, this girl *was not* happy about it. But her mom wouldn't let her off the hook, no matter how much she complained. Then the award letters started rolling in. By the time she started college, she had enough scholarships to give her a completely free ride for three years! That meant all she had to do was work enough during those three years to save up for her fourth year's tuition. That's incredible! What a great gift that mom gave to her daughter. It taught her about hard work, dedication, creativity, and, most of all, how several little scholarships lumped together add up to some serious cash.

Student Grants: Even More Free Money!

A college grant is basically a scholarship funded by the school, private individuals or institutions, or federal government assistance programs. Grants are usually based on need, and they may require your student to maintain a minimum GPA in order to keep receiving aid. Other than that, a grant is just like a scholarship, so your student should pursue every one you even think your family might be eligible for.

Stuck in the Details: Dealing with the FAFSA

The key to scholarship and grant money is the Free Application for Federal Student Aid (FAFSA). This is an excruciatingly long and detailed form that will make you wish you were filling out your taxes instead. Seriously, it's painful. That's the bad news. The good news is that the FAFSA opens the doors to all of the scholarships and grants your child will receive. In fact, it's required for practically any kind of financial aid.

You and your child need to sit down with the FAFSA form as early as possible during his senior year of high school. Those deadlines vary by state and school year, so get the most recent information at the FAFSA website (www.fafsa.ed.gov). Not long after you complete and submit the form, your student will get an award packet in the mail that outlines all of the scholarships, grants, and other assistance he or she is eligible for. This is where you need to be extremely careful, because it gets confusing. This packet will be filled with potential debt in the form of student loans. More often than you'd like to think, students mistake these loan offers for scholarships, so they turn in the requested paperwork and end up with a loan they never expected or wanted. Work with your child to make sure he's only applying for free money, not a pile of debt.

Make the Grade: ACT and SAT Prep

Dave: The higher your ACT or SAT scores, the more scholarships you qualify for. So your high schooler should plan on taking the tests at least twice, maybe three times. They should take an ACT or SAT prep class before each test to help raise their scores. There are a ton of test preparation businesses out there that can help. There are even firms that promise an improved score or they don't charge you for the class. Each of my three children took the ACT multiple times with prep classes between each test. In every single case, they improved their scores. It is worth the time and work if it means you will get more money for college.

GET A JOB: WORKING THROUGH COLLEGE

Rachel: As Dad and I talk to parents about having their kids work while they're in college, we hear all kinds of objections. Some of them are legitimate, but others are ridiculous. Let's take a look at the top three we've heard from parents.

"But My Child's Grades Will Suffer if He Works"

That's a myth, and it's usually held by parents who think their little darling does nothing but sit in the campus library all day absorbing the wisdom of the ages and staying five weeks ahead of his class deadlines. Please allow me to bust this myth for you. Your college student isn't spending eight hours a day resting and sixteen hours a day studying.

A part-time job will actually not hurt your child's grades; it will improve them. Studies show that students who work ten to nineteen hours a week actually have higher GPAs on average than students who don't hold jobs while in school.[6] There are even studies that show how much a student's GPA goes up the more he is responsible for paying for his education.[7] This might seem counterintuitive, but think about it: You value what you pay for, remember? We saw that when we talked about buying a car. If your child is financially invested in his own education, he's more likely to place a higher value on it and work harder to make the most of it. And if he's managing a job while in college, he also gets the added bonus of learning things like priorities, goal setting, and time management. That's some of the best education you can get in college.

"But I Want My Child to Enjoy College"

Dave: Someone please call the waaambulance. Seriously, sometimes I think we have lost our minds in this culture. All of you who worked while you were in school please raise your hands. Yep, that probably includes you. And you enjoyed college, right? I rest my case. The idea that it's child abuse for your children to work while in college is just nuts. They don't have to work, but it sure won't hurt them if they do.

We made our kids save for their cars, and we saved for their college, so we paid 100 percent of the cost of college for our children. This gift, however, was contingent upon them behaving like responsible adults, maintaining good grades, and graduating in four years. Our girls were involved in campus activities like sororities and Young Life and did not work outside jobs, which was fine with us. My son chose to work most of the time while he was in school to earn extra spending money and gain experience. He also was involved in Young Life. All of our kids maintained good (not perfect) grades and good behavior, and they all graduated in four years.

"But My Child Can't Cash-Flow College on a Part-Time Income"

Rachel: If your child has zero savings, no scholarships or grants, and a part-time job, then yes, he's going to have trouble starting college tomorrow. I'll give you that one. But let's get out of this mindset that school is year-round. It's not; it's usually broken up into two sixteen-week semesters a year. That leaves your child twenty weeks every year to work forty hours a week to pile up tuition money. Twenty weeks of working forty hours at ten bucks an hour is $8,000 before taxes. And remember, the average in-state tuition at a public university is only $8,655 per year. Throw in some part-time work during the fall and spring semesters, and it starts to look like your student really could work his way through school.

There's another issue we must deal with here, and that's the issue of timing. If your high school graduate waits until August to start thinking about how she's going to pay for college, then she may have to face the hard reality that she has to put school on hold for a semester. That may seem harsh, but trust me, it's a lot more gracious than walking her into student loans that will follow her around for years after graduation. I don't want your child to have to delay school, but sometimes it's necessary. That's another reason why you should start having these conversations with your kids while they're still in high school.

MANAGING THE COLLEGE LIFESTYLE

Movies and TV paint this amazing picture of what college life is like. You see students living together in huge apartments and going out to eat all the time, and no one ever seems to leave the party early to go to work. Reality, however, is a different story. Some dorm rooms are nasty. Many college-area apartments are gross. And you're never going to see meal-plan cafeteria food on the menu at the Four Seasons. Many students are so shocked by the reality that they go into an unbelievable amount of debt to bring their lifestyle up to the level they expected. They even use student loan money to supplement their lifestyle. That's such a big mistake. Even more than watching tuition and necessary expenses, keeping a handle on your students' college lifestyle could be the key to getting them through college debt free.

By the time he starts college, your child should have $500 in the bank for emergencies, and he should definitely be living on a budget. Even if you're still giving him money for expenses every month, he should be responsible for managing that money. If he calls home every other week asking for more money, you've got a problem. You might need to sit down with him and look at how he is spending his money. A lot of students don't take into account all of the expenses associated with college. He might be paying more for housing than he realized, so look at on-campus versus off-campus options. Food is always the top category college students spend their money on, so look at meal plans versus buying groceries. Even extracurricular activities come at a cost. Clubs, sororities, fraternities, intramural sports, season passes to their school's sporting events, and other activities will have fees attached. So it may not be that your student is blowing all of his money; it might be that he didn't take into account all the expenses associated with being a college student. So help him plan his cash flow—and don't be his on-call ATM.

Room and Board

Dave: You have to guard against the college lifestyle costing more than the education itself. An expensive car and an apartment with a Jacuzzi, a skylight, and a racquetball court aren't necessary to get an education. In most cases, dorm lodging and cafeteria food will work just fine. When I was in school, I lived at my grandparents' lake cabin for free. It had no heat except for a fireplace the first winter we lived there, so when we woke up in the morning, we could see our breath. Don't feel too sorry for me, though. I was living with a bunch of guys. It was an adventure, it was free, and it was on the lake. Once winter was over, we all thought we were in heaven!

Finish in Four Years

I worked my way through school with some help from family, and I graduated in four years because I didn't want to write any more checks than I had to. I watched the classes I needed to complete my degree like a hawk. I wanted out of there!

Given my personal history, I had a rude awakening sitting with my oldest daughter, Denise, at her college freshman orientation. The woman leading the orientation was standing in front of this group of people, bragging that the university's graduation rate was above the national average. The graduation rate was something like 53 percent which meant 47 percent of students didn't graduate. I couldn't help thinking to myself that the 47 percent of students who don't graduate leave school with student loan debt but no degree.

She continued to tell us that only 27 percent of graduates do so in four years. So only 53 percent of students actually make it to graduation and only 27 percent do so in four years. That means of those who start school, only 14 percent of incoming freshmen will graduate in four years, and she was bragging about it. I reached across to Denise's notebook and wrote, "So have a freaking plan!" If your child does not have a plan and follow it like her life depends on it, you (or she) will pay for it. And don't forget, colleges are in the business of making money. They will try to convince you that the four-year plan isn't realistic anymore. Don't buy it! Earning a college degree in four years *can* be done.

DREAM BIG

Rachel: I believe the two keys to graduating debt free are pretty simple: hard work and preparation. That's true whether we're talking about the parents' ability to save up over time in an ESA or 529 or whether we're talking about the student's dedication to filling out scholarship applications and earning his own money. Your child *can* afford to go to college, but it's not going to happen by accident—and student loans are *not* the answer. Remember, the only thing a student loan offers is short-term gain for long-term pain.

I'd rather your child be like Kristina Ellis, author of the great book *Confessions of a Scholarship Winner.* Growing up, Kristina and her family lived below the poverty line for years, and it was clear her mom wouldn't be able to write a check for Kristina's college education. On Kristina's first day of high school, her mom sat her down and told her she'd have to figure out what she wanted to do with her life. Her mother promised to take care of her until she graduated high school, but after that, she'd be on her own.

What I love about this story, though, is that Kristina's mom didn't stop there. Even though they were living in poverty, this amazing mother encouraged her daughter to dream big. Together, they set a goal for Kristina to earn enough in scholarships to go to a private college for free. She had four years to work on this goal, and she thought about it every day. Kristina wasn't a star athlete or genius-level brainiac either. Athletic scholarships weren't an option, and she was a decent student with average test scores. She didn't think she would get *any* scholarship money, but she never gave up the dream. She attended tutoring sessions before school to bring up her grades, and she started participating in after-school activities to round out her high school life. Her schedule began at 5:45 a.m. and ended at 9:00 p.m., but she never quit. In fact, she only got more and more focused.

She poured her heart into every detail of every scholarship application, knowing every dollar she received in scholarships meant fewer hours she'd have to work while in college.

Late in her senior year, the rejection letters started coming in. *Lots* of them. But guess what? She also received award letters—*unbelievable* award letters. One of the scholarships she won was for $20,000. Two other big ones came in from Coca-Cola and the Bill and Melinda Gates Foundation. Every day, she'd open the mailbox to find several rejection letters and a few key award letters. All of her hard work was paying off! She not only earned enough in scholarships for a free ride at Vanderbilt University, but she also had enough left over to pay for a master's degree at another private university. In all, Kristina earned more than $500,000 in scholarships. Can you imagine that? In high school, this one young lady—an average student with a single mom living in poverty—worked hard enough to earn half a million dollars!

The money is out there for your child to go to college. The process isn't easy and it isn't fast, but it's free and available to every student who bothers to give it a shot. It doesn't matter if your child is in preschool or high school, whether you have $200,000 in an ESA or just $20 in your savings account, your child *can* go to college debt free.

CHAPTER NINE

Contentment
The War for Your Child's Heart

Dave: Some of my favorite films are war movies. And no, it's not just because I enjoy watching explosions or people fighting each other (although the action doesn't hurt). The main reason is that I like to see a group of people fighting for something they actually care about—something worth fighting for. The goal is clear, and the enemy is in sight. There's a passion and conviction in those stories you rarely see anywhere else. When I hear William Wallace's call to arms in *Braveheart,* I want to march into battle with him. I want to grab a sword and shield and fight for freedom—for something that really matters.

When the stakes are high and the cause is just, good men and women are inspired to go to war. They are willing to stand up and fight to the finish, if that's what it takes. Well, I'm going to let you in on a little secret: If you are raising children in North America today, you are at war.

Whether you want to be or not, whether you realize it or not, you are at war with contemporary culture. The prize is not land, money, or possessions; this war is raging for the hearts of your children. Recognizing the reality and the seriousness of the war—and what is at stake if you lose—is necessary if you hope to have a shot at winning.

The heart of your child is under siege by endless marketing, pervasive peer pressure, and a choking shallowness from our contemporary culture. You can't take this attack lying down. You have to rise up and fight continuously and fiercely to protect your child from these enemies.

IT'S WILD OUT THERE

We live in the most marketed-to culture in the history of the world. We are hit by more advertising impressions in a few hours than previous generations experienced in an entire year. Please understand: I am not against marketing or advertising. I use them with my products. But we must understand that the very purpose of marketing is to make you think your life is somehow incomplete without the purchase of a product or service. The essence of marketing is to make you dissatisfied with the status quo, moving you in the direction of a purchase that will supposedly relieve a manufactured psychological tension. This dissatisfaction has a name: discontentment.

Buyer Beware
Since we live in the most marketed-to culture in the history of the world, it is possible that we live in one of the most discontented cultures in history as well. In our *Financial Peace University* class,

we teach a lesson called *Buyer Beware*, where we explore this discontentment and how it affects our purchases. Studies show that on average, the more advertising you are exposed to, the more debt you are in, so there *is* a correlation between the amount of TV you watch and the amount of debt you have. Why? Because you are being sold and sold and sold more "stuff."

As adults, we see how this discontentment leads to more purchases and more debt. We know it is bad—really bad. But when it begins to affect the hearts of our children, it reaches the point of near-evil. Your child is assaulted with marketing from the time he can process information. Advertisements between cartoons, a toy industry trying to meet quarterly profit projections, and parents asleep at the wheel are leaving the most vulnerable hearts open to the deadly disease of discontentment.

Happy Holidays?

The most persistent and sophisticated marketing is reserved for children. Think about how profitable "holidays" have become. Virtually every holiday now comes with mandatory kid purchases. Last year, Americans spent $8 billion on Halloween.[1] Whatever happened to dressing up in some old clothes and getting simple treats from a neighbor? Marketing and profits have turned Halloween into an industry. And don't even get me started on Easter or birthdays. Some parents and grandparents spend more today on a child's birthday than we spent on a whole family's Christmas a generation ago.

Companies know if they can plant the need or desire in a child's mind, they have employed the world's best salesman to sell their product to Mom and Dad. There is nothing as relentless as a kid motivated to have "the next great thing."

There's Always an Upgrade

Rachel: The ever-changing worlds of technology, cars, and fashion are probably the best examples of struggling with "the next great thing." This is something that's true with kids of all ages—even "kids" of retirement age! It seems like a fast new phone, gadget, or clothing style comes out every day, and the gotta-have-it fire is spread by more than just TV commercials. As tech companies try to outdo each other, their latest products become actual news. From cable news to blogs, people love to report on the shiny, new thing from Apple, Samsung, Toyota, and other companies. They play out a very weird, very public game of trying to outdo each other, and the media, from marketers to reporters, give them the biggest stage possible.

I know a guy who loves to watch Apple's big product announcements. He tries to stay uninformed all day long so he can rush home and watch the full video of the event without having it spoiled by headlines or talk around the office. Personally, I think that's crazy, but he loves it. I asked him why it was such a big deal, and he said, "I love their products, and I know I'll probably end up getting whatever they announce. So I basically watch the event to find out what they're going to make me buy each year."

I thought that was a pretty profound, honest (and, yes, kind of sad) statement: "to find out what they're going to make me buy." This is a grown man who handles his money really well—except for a particular weakness for pretty much anything this one company sells. He even admits he absolutely loves his iPhone from the day he buys it until the day the *next one* is announced. At that point, his current phone starts to look old and feel slow. The very announcement of the next cool thing somehow robs him of the joy of the cool thing he already owns.

When I talk to teenagers, I tell them that if the newness of stuff is what funds their happiness, they are going to be a rat in a wheel for the rest of their lives. They will keep going around and around, thinking the *next* thing is the thing that will make them happy. But of course it won't, so they just spin in circles, wasting all their time and energy and ultimately going nowhere. We live in a world where bigger is better and newer is nicer. But here's the truth: There's *always* an upgrade. There will always be a new "next great thing" fighting for your child's money and attention.

And as you can tell from my friend, the crazy Apple guy, contentment isn't about age; it's about maturity. I have met eighteen-year-olds who get this and forty-eight-year-olds who don't. Contentment isn't a money issue, even though it has a huge financial impact on your child's life. It's a *heart* issue. It's an example of how so many people try to fill a void in their hearts by cramming it full of more and more stuff. As the parent, you've got to prepare your child to defend himself against this threat.

The Best Protection

Dave: If you want to raise money-smart kids, you have to raise kids who are content. Yes, I know this is easier said than done. When I say you have to raise content children, your heart may skip a beat because you realize the war I am discussing is very real. But if you can foster a spirit of contentment in your children while they are under your roof, you have purchased the best insurance policy that they will win at life and money as adults. A content person can save, budget, avoid debt, handle relationships, and give exponentially better than someone who struggles with discontentment. The Bible says, "Godliness with contentment is great gain" (1 Timothy 6:6 NKJV). In our adult class series *The Legacy Journey,* we call the lesson on contentment *The Law of Great Gain*. This is one of our most popular lessons because contentment is something we all yearn for in our lives. We want to know how much is "enough" and how much is "too much" for our families. People with a right view of God's ownership want to make sure they don't fall off the cliff into discontentment as their income and wealth grow. We thoroughly explore these issues in that class because, for the past two decades, we've encouraged people to discover the keys to financial peace and contentment.

In a nonstop, frenetic culture like ours, sometimes we confuse contentment with a lack of ambition, or we may mistake contentment with apathy. Those traits do not reflect contentment at all. Ambition is not even on the same spectrum with contentment. Contentment is a spiritual experience that allows peace in the middle of a storm, but that peace isn't necessarily passive. It may very well be active. A content person still wants to *do* better and *be* better; he's just not pinning all his hopes and dreams on that one thing. He may say, "If this is all I ever have, I'll thank God and call myself blessed. But if I can grow and change and make a bigger impact on the world, then I'm going to do that." A content person doesn't avoid making decisions; he just doesn't feel the pressing need to make rash or stupid decisions. It is not necessary to be stagnant or unmoving to be content. So content people may not *have* the best of everything, but they *make* the best of everything. That is who you want your children to be.

It's Not an Amount

Rachel: I love that line: Content people may not *have* the best of everything, but they *make* the best of everything. That speaks volumes to a child. Contentment isn't based on an amount or how nice your stuff is. You may know some families who make $50,000 a year and are debt-free with a fully funded emergency fund and big retirement accounts, and you may know other families who make $150,000 who are deeply in debt with no savings and no retirement. Some of these families are looking for contentment in their income and possessions, but they'll never find it there. Contentment happens on the inside, and when you have it, it's there no matter how much money you make or how much stuff you have.

HOW TO WIN THE WAR

Dave: We have established that there is a war in our culture for the hearts of our children. Left unchecked, the cultural forces will steal your children's hearts and make them believe the lie that life consists of the stuff or experiences we buy. My goal here is to stir you up—to get you mad enough to go to war with that culture and win your child's heart to contentment.

No Mercy

The first thing to remember in this war is to show the enemy no mercy. When the enemy known as Discontentment breaks through your battle lines and takes hold of your child's heart, you must stomp Discontentment mercilessly until he is no more. The infection of this germ warfare is very dangerous, and you can give the enemy no quarter. At the first sign of a discontented spirit in your child, you must surgically remove it. You must act immediately, with precision and without mercy, knowing that your loving motive is to save the heart of your child.

When peer pressure, marketing, or a materialistic culture threatens the heart of your child with discontentment, you must squash it immediately. Remind your kids that owning stuff is fine, but when your stuff owns you, when you define yourself by a purchase or an amount of money, you are on the road to becoming a disgusting human being. We are not at war with success, but the words your children use and their emotions around a particular transaction will tell you whether this is a healthy goal or whether they are trying to define themselves by owning the iPhone 73 "that everyone else has." One clue to determining whether this is a healthy goal or a toxic identity issue is to see how old they act when discussing the purchase. If they respond appropriately for their age, it is likely healthy. But if they act three to five years younger than they are, then you know this is a toxic identity issue. When a thirteen-year-old acts like a four-year-old, then you know something is out of balance, and you must pounce.

Don't Join the Enemy

The second thing you must do to win the war for contentment is to recognize you can't *defeat* the enemy if you are *part* of the enemy. You can preach to your child all day long about not finding their identity in "stuff," but if you are defined by your car, your latest trip, or your purse, your kid is going to follow your example and not your sermon. Rachel has said several times, "More is caught than taught." There's a reason for that: It's true. If you are part of the culture of materialism, then you are siding with the enemy, and the war effort is doomed. You are heading toward defeat.

I am not suggesting a minimalist lifestyle or that you can't enjoy some nice things you have worked for, saved for, and paid cash for. I am saying your child knows where your heart is regarding those things. If your new car gets scratched, do you have a complete nervous breakdown? If so, you are sending a message to your child—not about new cars but about the worship of new cars. There is a difference, however, between caring for and maintaining things versus worshiping things. Don't we all remember an item our parents or grandparents had that was a prized possession? We all knew the emotional dynamite that was attached to that piece of "stuff." We don't want children to be out of control, breaking the family china. And we don't want children to become adults who don't maintain and care for things. But if Mom has to spend a weekend in the psych ward over a broken vase, then Mom has problems; it is not a vase problem.

So a major step to winning the war is to remember your children are going to define happiness, contentment, joy, and their identity the way you do. You can't defeat materialism in your kids if you are infected by it yourself. Search your heart and use the nobility of changing your family tree as motivation to clean up your discontentment act.

Teachable Moments

I really resist teaching life lessons to children by using a set curriculum taught only on Tuesday nights. Instead, Sharon and I always watched life unfold around us and our kids, and we looked for natural entry points to teach a lesson—a teachable moment. This is a third way to fight the war for contentment. Look for people who have lost the war—who define themselves by stuff and are living really shallow lives. When one of your child's friends or one of your friends or even a family member is losing the contentment war in front of your child, discuss it with your child at the first opportunity. Ask your child questions about what she observed. You will be shocked at how philosophical a five-year-old can be. Be careful not to tear down the people involved, but make sure you destroy the idea that contentment comes from stuff. You are not teaching your child to gossip about Uncle Harry; you are asking if she saw how Harry was defined by his purchase.

At the same time, don't confuse a war for contentment with a war on success. When someone in your life gets it right and is able to enjoy a purchase, celebrate that success and point it out to your child.

Don't just look for teachable moments in other people's failures; you can also find them in the normal, day-to-day activities of your kids. When my girls were in middle school, they were always asking to go to the mall to hang out with their friends. They were thirteen-year-old mall rats, because possibly the most social animal on the planet is a thirteen-year-old girl. Occasionally, I was recruited to play taxi driver and take them and their friends to the mall. The ride over was anything but lacking in conversation. Wow, could they talk! But we had a ritual as I pulled up to drop them off at the mall entrance. I gave them all the dad safety warnings, then ended with my "happiness talk." I would ask them to pick me up something while they were in the mall. This thrilled them, because being sent on a mission actually gave them a real reason to be there. My request was always the same. I'd say, "Pick me up a box of happiness while you are in there. I know happiness must be in there, because you are always in there looking for it. There must be a store somewhere between Gap and the food court called The Happiness Store that boxes this stuff up and sells it because people of all ages, including thirteen-year-olds, are in the mall every day looking for it. So my only requirement for taxiing you is that you bring me a box of happiness." Of course, this embarrassed my daughters. They'd roll their eyes, and as they all walked off, one of their friends would say, "Your dad is so weird."

This made me happy because I was able to accomplish two goals. First, I was able to teach a lesson on what is real and what can't be purchased. And second, I got to embarrass a teenager—every parent's dream.

Change Their Perspective

Rachel: The fourth way to fight back against discontentment is to show your child how blessed she is no matter how much she does or doesn't have. That's a perspective I gained while volunteering in Peru. One of the best gifts Mom and Dad gave us Ramsey kids was the chance to go on foreign mission trips. I took my first trip to Peru when I was twelve, and the experience was definitely an eye opener. It was the first time in my life I came face to face with complete poverty, meeting boys and girls my age who had practically nothing. That first trip made a huge impact on how I viewed my life and especially my stuff.

It was my second trip to Peru, though, that really changed me. I was seventeen at the time, and I noticed something about the people I met there: They were happy. No, not just happy; they were filled with joy and contentment, even though they probably couldn't even comprehend all the comforts I took for granted every day. I struggled with that for the first few days of the trip. I thought, *How can they be so joyful with nothing while I struggle with discontentment with so much?* During that trip, my whole mindset changed. I began to wonder how my attitude and even my daily routine might change if I took a lesson from these new friends. I started to see what my life could be like if I weren't so concerned with getting the latest phone or a new jacket—if I kept my stuff and the pursuit of *more* stuff from being the center of my world.

Later in the trip, we served breakfast and lunch to a group of people living in a remote village. Between meals, we played games with the kids and led a Bible study for the adults. There was one precious girl who stuck to me like glue the entire day. She had tattered clothes, tangled hair, and dirt all over her face. What really stood out to me, though, was her smile. She had an amazing, bright, beautiful smile. Everywhere I went, she was right there at my side, chatting away. Of course, I couldn't understand most of what she was saying—my two high school Spanish classes didn't stand a chance of keeping up with her steady stream of girlish excitement. That excitement hit its peak when I pulled out a pack of stickers from my purse and handed it to her. It was simply a pack of purple stickers you'd find for a few bucks on the rack at any Target store, but to this girl, it was a sacred treasure. She tore into the pack and immediately covered her face and arms with them. Soon, we were surrounded by a group of children, all laughing and playing as they passed the stickers around. Watching all of this unfold and seeing how happy these kids were with something so simple is something I'll never forget.

That afternoon, as our group was packing up to leave, my new little friend ran up and handed me the tiny, dirty keychain doll she'd been carrying around all day. At first I didn't understand, and she was talking too fast for me to keep up. It finally dawned on me that she was giving me her toy. I said, "No, no! That's yours. You keep it." But she kept pressing it into my hand.

I turned to our translator, who said, "She wants you to have it. She says she doesn't need it anymore because she has you for a friend." That is the moment I realized how priceless contentment is—how meaningful it is to truly let go of all the stuff I *thought* mattered and focus on the things that really do.

I know that's a hard lesson to teach kids, so I encourage you to give your children opportunities to experience it for themselves. You don't have to send them off to Peru (although it's not a bad idea, if you can), but you should look for ways to get them out of their normal, everyday lives and show them what life looks like through someone else's eyes. For me, it made all the difference.

IDENTIFY THE STAGES

Dave: The enemy of contentment is not that smart, and he certainly isn't subtle. Discontentment will tear through your child's life like a bull in a china shop. The bad news is that a lot of stuff can end up broken. The good news, though, is that discontentment leaves a trail that you, as the parent, can follow. There are specific things to look for to see if you have discontentment breaking through your lines of defense. We call these the three stages of discontentment.

Stage One: Jealousy and Envy

The first stage you need to watch for is jealousy or envy. Watch how your child reacts when one of his friends receives a gift or makes a fun purchase. The perfect response would be to celebrate the friend's good fortune. If your child does that, you know he has a healthy view of contentment, and he can set goals for how he might work toward the same blessing. However, if toxic jealousy spills out, you know the enemy has broken through your lines. And worse yet is Jealousy's evil aunt, Envy. Jealousy says, "I want what you have." Envy is worse, because she says, "I want what you have, but I can't have it, so I don't want you to have it either." Envy typically occurs when jealousy is allowed to incubate and grow. Teach your child to celebrate the blessings of others and develop goals to achieve similar blessings. Jealousy and envy are the first signs you are losing the battle.

Stage Two: Anxiety

Once jealousy and envy set in, we often see the next stage of discontentment's heart infection: anxiety. When the heart begins filling with discontentment, children and adults start to fret over what they don't have. They live in a comparison game of life, always measuring their purchases and the quality of their lives against someone else's—and always coming up short. People at this level of discontentment are perpetually anxious, feeling like they never measure up, and they often suffer from a real lack of joy. Overall, they are very unhappy people.

Keep in mind that some outside messages caused this infection. So the cure is to cut off or, at the very least, cut back on the messages. If the message is coming from a little friend who never hears the word *no*, who defines himself by his stuff, and who is constantly bragging to your child about his latest purchase, you will have to take action to protect your child. Deny that little friend access to your child until you are certain those messages have stopped. This may sound harsh, but if you do not deal with the source of the infection, it will never heal, your child will be unhealthy, and you may lose the war entirely. Translation: I don't want my kids hanging out with shallow, spoiled brats who brag incessantly.

If the source of the infection of discontentment is marketing or advertising, pull the plug. Less TV will likely cure the patient. Find where your kids are getting the messages that cause the meltdowns and cut off the messenger—whether it's TV, the internet, video games, friends, or carpool buddies. If your child were hanging out with the wrong kind of friends, watching inappropriate shows, or visiting sites encouraging him to do drugs, you would cut it off if you were any kind of decent parent. Discontentment is a socially accepted drug problem in this culture, but not for you or your family. As a parent, you need to regard it as dangerous as drug addiction; act like it can destroy your child—because it can.

Stop It at the Source

Rachel: This is something I've seen a million times: People flirt with whatever it is that drives them into a crazy fit of discontentment. For some people, it's hanging out at the mall. For others, it's spending hours on the internet researching new gadgets or cars they can't afford to buy. For me, it was Facebook.

One night during my senior year of college, I was sitting in my apartment scrolling through Facebook, catching up on everything my friends were doing. I saw a status update from a friend who had recently taken a trip to Paris with her mom. She had posted a ton of pictures, so of course I started flipping through them. I saw shots of her eating at incredible restaurants, visiting all the art museums and tourist attractions, and enjoying the city with her mother. But the pictures that really got my attention were the ones with shopping bags in the background. I'm talking bags and bags of new clothes. And not just any clothes; these were high-end designer clothes with the logos big and bright on the front of the shopping bags. Before I realized it, thirty minutes had passed, and I had studied every picture not once but twice. By then, I was absolutely burning with jealousy.

I wish I could say I was a mature young woman who was

happy for my friend who had a great trip to Paris. But that's not who I was at that moment. Sitting there on my sofa that night, I was a five-year-old little girl whining and saying things like, "It's not fair. I want to go to Paris like she did. Why can't I go?" I'm embarrassed to admit it, but it's the truth. Then, after about two minutes of wallowing in those thoughts, it was as though all the conversations my parents had ever had with me about contentment woke me up from my selfish daze. I knew exactly what was going on: I had a jealousy problem brought on by comparing my life to other people's lives through Facebook. Problem identified. Solution? I deactivated my Facebook account right then and there.

Later, when I finally came back down to earth from my mile-high pity party, I couldn't believe I had allowed Facebook pictures to get me so worked up. I knew I had an incredible life, so why was I trying to compare it to other people's status updates and travel pictures? I realized Facebook was not good for me—at least not at that point in my life. At the time, I figured I'd just back away for a few days, but after going a little while without comparing my life to anyone else's life, it was actually extremely liberating. I didn't go back and reactivate my account for several years, and even now, I don't spend time endlessly scrolling through what other people are doing. Cutting off the source of the discontentment infection was the cure.

This is the world your kids are living in. Thanks to "reality" TV and social media, your children are growing up in a culture that feeds discontentment by giving your kids a steady stream of what everyone else has, what kind of vacations they take, how nice their houses are, what kind of cars they drive, and on and on. It's an endless comparison game, and it feeds discontentment. I'm not saying your teens shouldn't watch reality TV or have social media accounts (under your supervision), but I am saying you should be on the lookout. Talk to them about how easy it is to fall into the discontentment trap just by "innocently" looking through their friends' photos on Facebook. I've been there, and it's not a fun place to be.

Stage Three: Defining Themselves by Their Stuff

Dave: Remember in the movie *Jerry Maguire* when Tom Cruise's character says to his wife, "You complete me," and women everywhere melted? The last stage of the discontentment infection is when your child says to stuff, "You define me." If you are only what you own or what you purchase, you seriously aren't much—except shallow. In Thomas J. Stanley's wonderful book *Stop Acting Rich*, he describes a whole culture of "adults" who are unable to control their money and build wealth because they are always acting rich. They buy things they don't need with money they don't have to impress people they don't even like or might not even know. They just want to look good. Their need to impress others is driving them into the poorhouse. Like I said before, Texans sometimes refer to this as "big hat, no cattle." Who you really are doesn't matter so much as who you *appear* to be. People this shallow define themselves by their stuff, and their need to look good ends up ruining their lives.

I'll Be Happy When . . .

Rachel: I'd like to be able to say that, growing up in the Ramsey house, I never struggled with "stuffitis"—the pursuit of stuff to make me happy. But sometimes, discontentment snuck up on me. I vividly remember standing in a store with a friend at fifteen years old and saying, "Look at that jacket! I love it! If I could only get that jacket for this winter, I will be happy." So, on a whim, I bought it. And I did feel happy . . . for a little while. A few months later, I walked into *another* store and saw *another* jacket I wanted. I thought, *Oh wow! I was wrong before.* This *is the jacket that will make me happy!* So I bought that one too.

A year later, I was looking through my winter clothes and found both of those "perfect" jackets in my closet. Deep in the closet. Okay, stuffed all the way in the back of my closet with other clothes piled on top of them. When I saw those jackets laying there all crumpled up, the magic and excitement were suddenly gone. There were no lights shining down from heaven, no blinking neon signs flashing "Happiness Here" floating above them. They just looked like two old, forgotten, slightly out-of-style jackets. I didn't think twice as I scooped them up and threw them in the pile of other clothes destined for the consignment shop.

Those two jackets were supposed to make me happy, but they ended up buried under an avalanche of other clothes I hardly remember buying in the first place. At that moment, at sixteen years old, it hit me like a ton of bricks: *Stuff is not going to fulfill me!* It was a powerful moment because it brought me face to face with what Mom and Dad had been telling me all my life. I suddenly had a shift in my mindset where it wasn't just listening to what my parents were telling me; it was a principle that had played out in my own life. I think Mom and Dad could have told me that every day and I still wouldn't have truly understood what they meant until I had that "Aha!" moment while looking in my closet. So as you work with your child, it's important to continually reinforce this principle, but don't be so strict and rules-based that she can't make some discoveries (and mistakes) on her own.

As frustrating as it is for a parent, that experience is what really drives the lesson deep into a child's heart.

It's Not a Destination

Dave: As parents, of course we don't want to intentionally raise children who are so shallow that they define themselves by a purchase or an item. So how do we prevent it in the midst of a culture where it is virtually the norm? By being careful to celebrate the accomplishments and character qualities that enabled them to make the purchase, you are reminding your children that they are not defined by the abundance of their possessions. Purchases are always the result of a goal, not the end goal. Never let a child utter the words, "I will be happy when . . ." Contentment isn't a destination; it's not somewhere you're leaving from, and it isn't somewhere you're heading to. Contentment is a manner of traveling. It's an attitude of peace and joy where you are, even while you are working to be somewhere else.

FIGHTING FOR THE CURE

So we've identified the war. We've talked about how to fight it. We've identified stages of discontentment to look for in your children. And now we have great news: We have the antidote to the discontentment infection of the heart. The antidote is so strong that if you use it often enough, you can virtually ensure the heart will not become infected with discontentment. Drum roll . . . are you ready?

Gratitude.

A heart filled with gratitude leaves no room for discontentment.

Why is it that a two-year-old is often happier playing in the box a toy came in rather than playing with the actual toy? Why is it that children living in poverty in third-world countries seem happier and more content than kids in wealthy nations? Because neither is caught in the trap of comparisons. They don't know what they are missing out on. They are simply grateful.

Don't Raise Ugly Kids

Gratitude is really, really attractive. A child who is genuinely grateful makes you want to do anything for her, and that is true of adults as well. As parents, we've all experienced those wonderful, sweet, humbling moments when our children look at us with eyes filled with gratitude for something we've done for them. At that moment, they are the most beautiful, most precious children they could ever be. And sadly, most of us have had the opposite experience—seeing a child open a present and acting ungrateful. There are few things uglier than that. The child's attitude was so ugly, you may have threatened to return all the birthday or Christmas gifts as a reaction to the lack of gratitude.

My friend Zig Ziglar used to say you have to develop an attitude of gratitude. You have to learn to count your blessings. Have you ever thought about what you would pay for an eye if yours were put out? Have you ever thought about what you would pay to replace one of those amazing things you have at the end of each arm—that miraculous machine called a hand? We all have things to count as blessings, but we also have a tendency to lose our sense of awe and our sense of gratitude. Make sure your heart is full of gratitude for the blessings in your own life. Let your children witness this in you, and they will want to respond with gratitude for the blessings in their own lives.

The Source of Gratitude

So where does gratitude come from? What makes a child truly grateful? I believe gratefulness starts with humility.

When I talk about humility, I don't mean humiliation. These are two different things. Humiliation is all about shame or feeling embarrassed about something you've done. Humility is different. It is the opposite of entitlement, and it is the key to gratitude. James Ryle says, "Humility is the God-given self-assurance that eliminates the need to prove to others the worth of who you are, and the rightness of what you do." The bottom line is that humility struggles to exist in the discontented heart. And it is very hard for discontentment to take root in a heart filled with humility that gives way to gratitude.

Humility through Giving

Rachel: C. S. Lewis once said that humility is not thinking less of yourself but thinking of yourself less. See the difference? Like Dad just said, thinking less of yourself is humiliation, not humility. It says you've done something wrong or you're ashamed about who you are or what you've done. That's false humility. True humility is more about thinking of yourself less, taking the focus off yourself—what you do or don't have—and putting it on the needs of other people. The best way to nurture a spirit of humility and other-centeredness is to encourage a heart of giving in your child.

I want you to see the trail that runs from giving to humility to gratitude to contentment. It's a progression that leads your child out of the land of discontentment and toward an incredible life of joy and freedom. When your child is focused on meeting the real *needs* of others through giving, it becomes harder and harder for him to focus on his *wants*. As giving becomes a natural part of your child's character, you'll see his whole perspective change. Dad just said that it's hard for discontentment to take root in a heart filled with humility. In the same way, it's almost impossible for selfishness to flourish in the heart of a giver. With every act of giving, your child is taking a stand against discontentment. It's like he's saying, "I not only have enough for me, but I have enough to share with you." That's the fertile ground of contentment.

And again, it's not about age, it's about maturity. Some kids will get this quickly and easily, and others will struggle with it for a while. You can help direct them, but you can't force it. Give them guidance, but also give them grace.

Dave: Children deserve to be loved and to know they are loved. They deserve to be cherished and to know they are valuable. Unfortunately, our culture has embraced toxic views that undermine that noble end and foolishly prefers to give self-esteem classes to kids who can't read rather than to simply teach them to read. Our noble valuing of children has in some cases convinced our wonderful little savages that the axis of the world runs through the tops of their heads. We have become so kid-centric that our children have been robbed of humility, which prevents them from being grateful and opens them to lives full of discontentment. It is our job as parents to love our children so much that they learn their value while remaining humble. Humility is a valuable virtue because it breeds gratitude, which is unbelievably attractive and bodes well for your child's adult life. And, of course, gratitude is the best antidote to a lack of contentment. Have the courage as parents to fight this war for the heart of your child. Fight it daily, fight it fiercely, and keep fighting until you win!

CHAPTER TEN

Family

Put the FUN in Dysfunctional

Rachel: We've been talking about how to help your kids win with money throughout this book, and by now, you may have caught on to the secret of personal finance: Money is never *just* about money. Sure, you and your kids have to do the details—things like budgeting and keeping your checking accounts balanced—but there's so much more to consider. Winning with money also means getting comfortable doing some good, old-fashioned hard work. It means learning patience, delayed gratification, and contentment. It means developing the heart of a giver. Those are all key indicators of people who are on track to win with money long term. That's why Dad and I always say that personal finance is only 20 percent head knowledge; the other 80 percent is behavior. Knowing *what* to do is the easy part. Actually *doing* it and understanding *why* you're doing it is where it can go right or wrong.

With that in mind, there's a key indicator of most successful people that is often overlooked: quality relationships. It's hard to win with money and teach your kids how to handle money if dysfunction is pulling your family apart. You may think dysfunction is a strong word, or maybe you don't think it's strong enough for your situation, but let's be honest: All families are dysfunctional, at least a little. By "dysfunctional," I simply mean no family functions perfectly all the time. That's because there are no perfect families—and that includes the Ramseys. You know why there are no perfect families? Because there are no perfect people, and families are full of imperfect people. So the question isn't whether or not you've got a little dysfunction; the question is how you're going to address it.

Dealing with the different family systems and stresses is key for your child to win with money. The degree to which you address the dysfunction head-on is the degree to which your child will succeed with money. Every relationship in your child's life has enormous potential to bless her more than you can imagine. As the parent, you have the responsibility to manage who is coming in and out of your child's life and what they're bringing into it. That means you have to be intentional about who sets the table for your child's future.

Because we will cover a variety of family situations here, this chapter will look a little different than the others. We're going to discuss "conventional" families (with a mom, a dad, and 2.3 kids), single-parent families, families of divorce, and blended families. We're also going to talk about how adoption may fit into your family and finances, and we'll look at the unique budgeting concerns of families with special-needs children. We'll even cover the roles of grandparents—from grandparents who may excessively spoil a grandchild to grandparents who are actually raising a grandchild. Like I said, we're going to cover a lot in this chapter, so hang on!

GETTING THEM GROWN AND GONE

Before we dive in to look at each of the different types of families, we need to talk about why this even matters. What exactly are you trying to prevent or accomplish? Well, allow me to be extremely bold and direct here: You're trying not to raise spoiled, entitled, unmotivated kids who grow up to become spoiled, entitled, unmotivated adults who end up living at home with you. I think I speak for the rest of the world when I say we have enough of those young adults roaming around. We'd rather have more happy, successful, and productive members of society, so we're all rooting for you to raise money-smart kids! With that said, let's take a few minutes to identify exactly what happens when messed-up relationships and bad influences take over your child's life.

Dethroning the Princess Mentality

Dave: When it comes to dethroning a "princess," my best advice is not to have a throne or a princess in the first place. When I was growing up, if someone accused a child of being spoiled, it was a huge insult. Now, when people say a child is spoiled, it is often meant as a cute description of the child's "unique" personality.

The word "spoiled," when applied to anything else, means something has gone bad. If you bought food at the store and got home and realized it was spoiled, you would be upset with the store. If you ate spoiled food, you would get food poisoning and have a few miserable days. Spoiled things smell. They are rotting and decaying. They attract flies and other insects. Spoiled things turn dark and moldy. Have you ever opened some old milk that stayed in the refrigerator too long? Just thinking about it gives me a gag reflex. Spoiled is nasty. And spoiled children can give you that same reaction. No one wants to be in close proximity with anything that is spoiled—including your children.

Please don't misunderstand us. Neither Rachel nor I want anyone to create over-disciplined little robots who have their very spirits squeezed out of them. Children can be full of personality, poise, and confidence, and they can be a joy to interact with when they are simply given loving boundaries.

Spoiled Kids and Wimpy Parents

So what creates a spoiled child? We can all imagine what a brat looks, acts, and sounds like. He gets everything he wants, never hearing the word *no,* and he becomes entitled, ungrateful, and belligerent. His parents are weak-willed—wimpy—and the inmate begins to run the asylum. To avoid this insanity, we as parents simply must say no sometimes—and stick to it. We need to assert our control and command over our households. Don't think for a second that your children aren't smart enough to manipulate you. They are. And they will as long as you let them. As always, we need to look for teachable moments to communicate and model proper, respectful behavior to our kids.

When I was about ten years old, I was enamored with becoming a friend of the new kid at my school. He was confident and cool and wore a lime-green shirt that I still remember to this day. We soon became friends, and I was invited to his home to play one day after school. I was horrified as I listened to him yell at his mother, throw a fit, and boss her around like she was his servant. I had never witnessed anything like that. I just knew at any moment his mom was going to turn on him and kill him right there in front of me, which is what would have happened at my house. That level of disrespect, arrogance, and yelling at an adult would have resulted in instant death in my home—at least in my mind.

At that point my new friend no longer seemed cool to me. I lost all respect for him and for his wimpy mother. Some people might think this was simply a behavior issue, but the problem was this boy had never been told no. He was given everything he wanted every time he asked. He was a nightmare, and unfortunately he became a dark and depressed teenager because his parents refused to give him boundaries when he was a kid.

As a parent, let your yes be yes and your no be no. No is a complete sentence. It doesn't need an explanation. Have integrity. Stick to your answer. And enforce consequences for fits or negative outbursts that result from the healthy, loving boundary you set. Saying no and sticking to it takes tremendous energy in the moment. However, over the scope of your life, it takes less energy because nothing is more draining than an eight-year-old brat or a self-centered teen. Few things in life are more disheartening than watching your adult child fail in his relationships, finances, career, and every other area of life because you never set boundaries for him as a child. Saying no takes energy at the time, but it saves your life and your child's life in the long run.

From the time your children are small until they are completely on their own, your job is not to be their friend. Your job is to parent them. Trying to be BFFs with a fifteen-year-old is pitiful on your part and embarrassing for your child. Be a loving, kind, forgiving, firm, friendly parent, but don't be his or her friend. If you will parent well, your accomplished, dignified, grown children will become some of your best friends when the time is right.

Spoiled or Blessed?

Rachel: I said before that you must carefully manage how the relationships in your child's life impact him. That includes listening closely to any offhanded comments your own friends make to your kids. Soon after getting home from a family vacation one year, I had a conversation with one of Mom and Dad's friends about our trip. She said to me, "Oh, Rachel. You're so spoiled!" She didn't mean it to be rude or demeaning. I think it was just her way of telling me how fortunate I was to have the chance to go on a nice vacation with my family. But that word—*spoiled*—got stuck in my head for a while. I developed a habit of saying, "I'm spoiled," whenever I got to do something special or I received a nice gift.

Eventually, I said it to my parents during a dinner conversation. Dad cut me off mid-sentence and said, "Rachel, stop saying you're spoiled. You're not. Spoiled means something has gone bad. You kids are not spoiled because you have not gone bad. You're not spoiled; you're blessed."

That's a conversation I will carry with me the rest of my life because it did two things. First, it showed that Mom and Dad were paying attention to the influence their own friends were having in my life, and they were correcting any wrong ideas other adults were giving me. Second, it taught me the difference between being spoiled and being blessed.

Even today, as I interact with thousands of teens every year,

I can pick out the ones who are spoiled and the ones who are blessed. It's amazing that the same gift or opportunity can spoil one kid but bless another. It's all about the child's attitude. It's 80 percent *behavior*, remember? If they feel entitled to new clothes or a beach vacation, your kids can spoil quickly. But if they recognize everything they have represents the love and care of their parents, then you know they have the right spirit of gratitude and appreciation. They're blessed.

Entitlement and Ownership

As Dad's business became more successful, my parents became much more intentional about preventing any kind of entitlement mentality from creeping into their kids' hearts. One way they did that was to consistently remind us that we didn't own much of anything. They kept God's ownership in perspective, teaching us over time that we were stewards of God's resources, but they also emphasized that they were the ones who provided our home, clothes, food, and most of our possessions. For example, we weren't allowed to say to them, "Stay out of my room." It may sound silly, but Mom and Dad would reply, "Excuse me? You don't have a room. This is our house, and we're kind enough to let you borrow a little piece of it." It was never mean-spirited in any way; they just wanted us to remember that we weren't *entitled* to everything we wanted simply because we were their kids. Having individual bedrooms all to ourselves was a blessing, and it was one they didn't want any of us to take lightly.

The funniest reminder of ownership came when my brother was in fourth grade. Mom and Dad were several years out of bankruptcy at that point, and Dad's business had started to grow. The bankruptcy had really taken an emotional toll on my parents, though, and even at that point—when the financial crash was behind them and their income was picking up—you could still see some of the scars. Probably the most visible reminders were Dad's old cars. Ever since bankruptcy, he had driven old, cheap-but-reliable cars that were high on quality but low on luxury. Finally, one of the VPs at his company convinced him it was time to buy a nicer car. The fact that they had this discussion while broken down on the side of the road may have had something to do with it!

Dad was finally emotionally ready to buy himself a nice car again, and, of course, it was used and he paid cash. When he drove it home, the whole family piled in the car, and Dad took us for a drive around the neighborhood. It was the nicest car we'd had my entire life, which at that point meant there wasn't a hole in the overhead lining and the brakes didn't screech at every stop. When we got home and parked in the driveway, my brother, Daniel, reclined back as far as he could and stretched his arms out across the top of the backseats. With his chest puffed out, he said, "Man, Dad, we are doing *pretty good*."

Dad turned around from the driver's seat, laughed, and said, "*We're* doing pretty good? No, son. *I'm* doing pretty good. You guys got nothin'!" We love that story because it's a perfect example of the kinds of conversations that were common in our house. Our parents made it clear to us from an early age that we had no rights to their success. We weren't entitled to have more or do more simply because they were making more money. That meant when they did splurge on something, we saw it as a huge blessing. It changed our whole attitude about those special times, and we were able to enjoy the gift or vacation without feeling like it *should* have been bigger or better.

Enabling Disaster

Another problem parents run into is enabling. I know there are different definitions of enabling, so for our purposes I'm talking about parents doing everything for their kids and not giving their children opportunities to work, succeed, or fail on their own. In some families, a parent might enable a lazy student by doing his homework for him. In others, enabling may be stepping in and rescuing the child every time his bad decisions lead to painful consequences. Kids need these opportunities to grow, and yes, they need to feel some pain associated with their mistakes. It's how they avoid making the same mistakes in the future.

Probably the most common form of enabling that parents fall into is failing to say the word *no*. It may seem easier to quiet a screaming child by giving her whatever she wants, but over time, that establishes a pattern of rewarding bad behavior. Hearing and accepting the word *no* does something wonderful for your child: It teaches her boundaries. I heard Mom and Dad say no a lot—to me, to my brother and sister, and to themselves. That's a powerful thing to witness. Now, as an adult, I'm able to say no to myself when I want something I either can't afford or simply isn't a good idea. It's not always easy, and I'm certainly not always happy about it, but I know it's good for me so I do it anyway. Hearing the word *no* is an incredible gift my parents gave me from a young age.

Let's look at the opposite. If a parent gives a child free rein in the home her whole life, protects her from all pain, and rescues her from all the consequences of her bad decisions, the child will grow into a completely frustrated and confused adult. As a young woman, she won't understand the connection between work and money, and even worse, she won't understand the connection between bad judgment and bitter consequences. She'll spend years wondering why the world isn't bending over backward to give her what she wants.

As I've worked with teens and young adults, I've seen this many times, and it's always frustrating and heartbreaking. Bad behavior stemming from parental enabling has almost become a stereotype. I'll meet a guy in his mid- to late twenties. He has a college degree and can talk for hours about all the fun times he had in school, but he's currently unemployed and living with his parents. As I dig into his story, I'll discover his parents always did everything for him as he was growing up. He never had to work, he never heard the word *no*, and he basically never had to put much effort into accomplishing anything. His parents were always there to pick up his slack. And now, while most of his friends are already a few years into their careers, starting families, and generally being adults, this guy can't hold a job, lives with his parents, and is always complaining about how he can't catch a break. I'm sorry if that sounds harsh, but this is real life. I've met a lot of young adults in this exact situation, and it's not what I want for your child. Trust me, it's not what you want either.

Enabling is the enemy of motivation. Doing and providing everything for your child throughout her whole life leaves her totally unmotivated as an adult. Please hear me, though: I want you to bless your kids. I want you to throw big parties and give fantastic gifts when it's appropriate and fits in your family budget. But I want those parties and gifts and vacations to be blessings, not curses, to your children. When you give them the "stuff" without giving them the character to carry it, all those things you think are blessings actually pile up on your kids' backs and cripple them.

They can't stand up straight with dignity because they're always looking for the next thing they *deserve*. They're looking for the next handout, and they become adults who don't understand why people aren't crawling out of the woodwork to make their lives more comfortable. When that happens, you've got a train wreck on your hands, and that entitled, enabled young adult will likely end up living in your basement. And he may try to stay there forever!

Raising Arrows, Not Boomerangs

Dave: The psalmist said, "Like arrows in the hand of a warrior, so are the children of one's youth" (Psalm 127:4 NKJV). This is a great word picture to remind us that our children are to be released into the world. If they are strong and true, they will fly straight just like an arrow that is properly formed. It is gratifying to pull back a bow, let an arrow fly, and watch it strike the bull's-eye. Unfortunately, in our soft and wimpy culture, we are not releasing arrows; we are releasing boomerangs. We throw them out, and they come right back. A guy called the radio show one day saying he figured out how to prevent grown children from living in their parents' basements: Buy a house without a basement. In this book, we want to give you the tools you need to avoid having a forty-two-year-old child move back into your basement.

In the United States today, 19 percent of males ages twenty-five to thirty-four are living with their parents.[1] If this is because they are in college, then either they have been in school at least three years longer than normal or they are just returning to college. This statistic says one out of five young males have "failure to launch." We have an epidemic of young men in this country who refuse to act like men and stand on their own. They have never known the dignity of making their way in the world. It may seem mathematically efficient for your sons to live with you to "save money," but in most cases, this only creates a mess for them.

Safety Net, Not a Hammock

I am all for taking in a grown child temporarily when there is a crisis. Loving parents providing a safety net is a great thing. On the other hand, you should not allow the safety net to become a hammock used by a listless, lazy, unmotivated video-game expert.

When should grown children be allowed to live at home and under what circumstances? Well, that is certainly up to you, but the longer they are rescued, coddled, and enabled by you, the more their spirits will atrophy. They will become flabby and not have the character or the fight to win in the marketplace. I would suggest you only take this chance in extreme crisis and/or for short periods of time. If someone is recovering from a medical problem, divorce, drug addiction, or even a job loss, then temporary housing is reasonable. Moving home in order to save more money really should not happen unless, again, it is for a very short period of time.

The grown child rotting in your basement is spoiling. How do you know if you are enabling an adult child living at home? If he refuses to look for a job, he stays out late and sleeps in even later, and he doesn't do his own laundry or prepare his own food, then those are sure signs you have a parasite in your house. Too much TV and video-game time are other sure signs you have a serious problem on your hands.

If you allow your grown child to move home for a safety net while working through a crisis, you must be very specific about your expectations. First, you must put an agreed-upon time limit on how long he or she will be there. This deal is not in perpetuity.

Second, they must be taking steps to solve their crisis. If they are just hiding out from the world, you are not doing them any favors. I would not charge rent, but I would require personal behaviors that promote healing as your rent payment. Instead of rent, you might require they spend three hours a day on their job hunt, they do a budget and show it to you, they save a certain amount of money monthly, they exercise, and they keep good adult work hours, not party-animal hours. These types of things are for their good. They act as a net for safety, not a hammock for napping. Nets save you, but they are not comfortable.

Third, if they are in your home, they must act according to your value system and your rules. At our home, those rules would mean no drugs, no overnight guests sleeping in their bed, regular church attendance, coming home at a reasonable hour (we are not a college dorm), and pitching in by doing chores around the house. (By the way, I abide by those rules myself, and Sharon lets me stay.) And if they feel like all this is too controlling, they can find somewhere else to live. This is your home. You are being generous to allow them to stay as a guest, so they must use good manners and use this time to get their feet back under them.

UNDERSTANDING FAMILY TYPES

As Rachel and I travel the country teaching these principles, we are often asked questions about how to raise money-smart kids in certain family configurations. I want to drive by some of these types of families and look at a few things these specific households face. Before we do, you should understand that the things we have covered up to this point are essential to raising money-smart kids, and you don't get a free pass just because your situation is slightly different. Regardless of the nuances of your family, your children still need to understand the basic money skill sets, or they will struggle financially.

Conventional Families

Let's look at the so-called "conventional" or nuclear family—a father, a mother, and 2.3 kids all living in the home. That is how I grew up and how the Ramsey kids grew up. This household used to be the typical family, but conventional families are now in the minority. If this is your family, all we have talked about so far applies. I just have a few things for you to remember as parents.

First, communicate to your kids that while they are a treasure and you love them more than life itself, Mom and Dad are first. Your children need to grasp that they are second to your marriage. I was in love with Sharon before my kids were even a thought, and she is still here now that they are all grown and gone. That was always the plan, and our kids knew it. Dad's first priority is Mom, and Mom's first priority is Dad. This sets the table nicely for Mom and Dad to teach and lead the children through the life lessons of handling money. Oddly enough, in homes where this concept is understood, the children feel very secure and are more confident.

Second, the parents must present a unified front. This is a battle with two big people against the little people for the good of the little people. Your sweet, little savages are experts at the divide-and-conquer strategy. If Dad and Mom don't both enforce chores and the principles of giving, saving, and spending, the children will not take them seriously. It would be very difficult for only one parent to teach the smart money kids' concepts and have them stick. So make a pact as parents that you are going to do this as a unified front and have each other's back.

Maintain a Unified Front

Rachel: I think every parent has a particular phrase that really gets his or her child's attention more than anything else. It's different for every family, and I promise your kids know what yours is. Whatever it is, when your children hear *that phrase*, it stops them in their tracks. They know they're in for it—that they've pushed the boundaries a little too far. For my dad, that phrase was, "*Never* talk to my wife that way!" If you ever heard that phrase in our house, you can bet there was a Ramsey child in some serious trouble, because it meant one of us had done the unthinkable: We had talked back to or disrespected our mom.

When I was young, I always thought it was weird that Dad would get so worked up about that. In my little-kid mind, Sharon Ramsey was my mom. That's it. That was my whole perspective. I couldn't figure out why Dad got so upset when we gave Mom "attitude." But now, looking back at those moments warms my heart. As an adult, I realize he was a man protecting his wife from someone who was treating her poorly—even if that someone was their own child. What a message to send your children! Denise, Daniel, and I knew Mom and Dad were a team, and trying to get between them or play one against the other was the worst mistake we could make. Dad always made it clear that no matter how much he loved us, his first priority was his wife.

It was a more powerful example to me than I had even realized. As an adult, subconsciously, one of the big reasons I fell in love with my husband was because he was a man who would stick up for me no matter what. If you're married and you and your spouse are raising a child together, it is critically important for both of you to present a unified front to your kids. They may not always like the results, but in the end, it develops stability and security in your family.

Single-Parent Families

Dave: The single parent who is raising children alone has a tough fight. In this section, I am not going to address situations where another parent is still involved. That will come later. This is for the single mom or dad who is going it alone because of the death of a spouse, a divorce where there is no further contact, or simply any reason that the other parent is not there.

If this is your situation, you must continue to teach all the lessons discussed in this book and follow the principles. They do not change because of your circumstances. But there are two additional—and critical—things you have to do to make sure you raise money-smart kids. First, stand your ground, and don't let your kids try to convince you that you are wrong just because they outnumber you or because they know you don't have a spouse to back you up. Once you decide to implement sound money-management principles, you can expect a rebellion among the small savages. They will try to convince you that you have lost your mind and that joining this cult was a bad idea. The single parents I have coached often suffer from battle fatigue because they are substantially outnumbered. Take this as your reminder: Just because you are the only adult in the house does not make you wrong. As a matter of fact, it usually makes you right. So resist the claims that you are an overbearing tyrant when it comes to money; be strong, persist, and grow money-smart kids.

Second, if you are going it alone on the parenting front, you should call in reinforcements. It's essential to surround yourself with a community that is in agreement with your goal to raise money-smart kids. You can't do it alone. A guy recently called my radio show and told me that he and his wife had been working our system for fifteen years. They had become debt-free and wealthy. He said the most rewarding part is that he is now mentoring his ten-year-old niece and fourteen-year-old nephew on money. They are being raised by his sister (a single mom), but both kids asked the aunt and uncle how they can become wealthy like them. This single mom has reinforcements. You may not have a rich sister or brother, but you can bring in youth pastors, extended family members, and friends to help you out. You could even adopt an older couple who are empty-nesters to act as surrogate grandparents in your money-smart kids program. Let your little community know what you are teaching in detail so they can reinforce the messages and lessons.

Parenting after Divorce

When both parents are still involved in the kids' lives after a divorce, sadly they seldom work together for the good of the children. Obviously the best scenario is one where both households, parents and stepparents, are all unified in the goal of raising the kids well and teaching them to be money-smart. Both families should read this book and follow the principles so you can have commission worksheets in both households and a plan for car purchases and college that both households are in agreement on.

If your former spouse is unwilling to cooperate, you already know you are in an uphill battle on all aspects of raising your children. It's really confusing for children to have two different value systems sending two different messages. But you can't control what the other parent does. Implementing money-smart kid principles is no different than the other areas of disagreement. You can only control what happens in your home. Our suggestion is to avoid trashing the ex but to firmly apply the principles in your home. You no longer have 100 percent influence, but you will do what you can do in your home.

As the stakes get higher in the teen years, I suggest you make it clear to your teen and even your former spouse that you will not be supporting or financing decisions you do not agree with. If the ex suggests that your children take out student loans for college and is willing to cosign for loans at a school that you don't agree with and isn't affordable, you are under no obligation to release the college fund you have saved. The same thing holds true for cars. Your message must be clear: You buy the car without debt, or you can't drive it while living here. You go to a school I agree with and you can afford, or you get no money or help from me. It may sound harsh, but when your teen hears you firmly but kindly explaining the money-smart principles again and sees you sticking to them, he will be able to avoid huge mistakes.

Be prepared: You will be made out to be the bad guy, but you are the only one in the whole picture who is using your brain. Every parent is tested frequently to see if what we want is smart and best or whether we will cave and let our kids do something we know is a bad idea. After a divorce, a parent still deals with that same test but with more emotion and less support for the stand you take. Take the stand anyway. Do what is right for your child, even if no one understands.

Guilt Spending

We mentioned the Disney Dad concept in Chapter 3—the idea that one parent buys everything in sight for the kid while the other parent is left looking like the troll because he or she actually uses common sense. A friend of mine who was a good dad went through a divorce that was his fault. He messed up, and his family fell apart. This dad, who used to have good judgment and who guided his children well, became Disney Dad. He bought the kids too many clothes, let them eat and watch anything, took them to Disney (hence the nickname), and generally spent all his income and time with his kids in the wrong ways. After a couple of years, we sat down to look at his messed-up financial picture. He had tons of credit card debt all because of how he was spending on his kids post-divorce. He made a profound statement that began his healing and led to him becoming a much better dad. He said, "You can't spend your way out of guilt." His guilt from his failed marriage was driving his unwillingness to say no to his kids. When he realized this and changed his actions, he was able to turn his whole life around.

Disagreeing on Schools

In Chapter 8, we discussed private versus public K–12 education. It is worth noting here that in a divorce situation, one parent can have strong feelings about private versus public schools that the former spouse does not agree with. In most divorce situations, the incomes are now split into two households and, in many cases, there is simply not enough money for private school to be an option. Unless your divorce decree or the judge says you are required to fund a private education, the decision is up to you, not your ex. Just make sure you can afford your decision.

The same is true for funding your child's college. Unless you have a court-ordered decree, you get to decide what you will do, and you should never go along with bad decisions coming from your former spouse. Once your marriage partner became your former spouse, you were freed from participating in his or her stupidity.

Child Support

Children are to be cared for by adults. Child support is the law in every state, and it should be. I know there are cases where child support is mishandled by the court or the opposing attorney and it becomes a crazy, confusing situation, but there are many more cases where the supporter does not do what he or she is supposed to do regarding care for their own children. This is despicable. Children are cared for first in your budget before you do anything for yourself. And if you marry someone who has children from a previous relationship, you are agreeing to the fact they have children to support. It is ridiculous for you to marry someone with children and then gripe and whine that they pay child support. It is the right thing to do, and it is the law.

Blended Families

In a traditional nuclear family where all the children are biologically yours, you have to really take care that your children don't divide and conquer you and your spouse. Since we know kids try to do this in a traditional family, you can certainly expect that the blended family is a divide-and-conquer battle waiting to happen. Many blended families do a great job of providing a healthy environment and avoiding the Cinderella Syndrome, allowing the stepmother/stepfather to be a loving parent as opposed to being cast in the bad-guy role. Every couple considering marriage should get premarital counseling, but you are really asking for trouble if you don't get some coaching in advance when heading into a blended-family marriage.

There are too many possible his/her/our scenarios to give each one attention in this chapter, so let's look at some basic things that must be in place for you to teach your kids money-smart concepts and make them stick.

Children under the age of eighteen are to be cared for, loved, and guided by the big people. All the children are to be loved by all the adults.

If your children think they are more important to you than your spouse, they will use that to destroy any chance of you leading them well. They will immediately begin a campaign that says the stepparent is evil.

The bottom line is that you have to love and care for all the children under your roof and, while doing that, put your marriage first, or you will quickly create a toxic household. If there are two classes of children in the house, they will realize it and take advantage. Yours, mine, and ours must be treated the same. They all learn to work, they all learn to save and give, and they all learn the money-smart kid principles we have been talking about. If you are unwilling to finance your future spouse's minor children's lives at the same level you are financing your own, you should not marry.

Once the children realize they are all treated the same and that you can't be played against your former spouse, you will have a loving household where you can apply teaching for their future. If you are receiving child support, you are likely spending more than that amount to take care of your child. If that is the case, then there is no need to separate the child support and bank it separately. It is for the care and feeding of the child; it is not the child's money. Since the care and feeding are happening, then there is no moral, ethical, and certainly no legal reason to keep those funds separate from the family budget. One big pile of income and one big pile of family expenses keep all the children on equal footing. If, however, an ex-spouse were to pass away and an estate is left to those children, that money should be kept separate and held for when they become adults.

Adult children should always be told and taught that they are responsible for taking care of themselves and they have no moral rights to your estate. If you have minor children, they and your spouse are the main concern of your estate. After your current household is taken care of, the grown children might be included if you have more money. But your spouse and minor children are your first priorities. Again, fair does not always mean equal.

Adoption

Adoption is a beautiful thing—whether you are adopting to start your family, complete your family, or give a child a much-needed home. Adoption is not for everyone, but those people who respond to that tug at their hearts are greatly rewarded. But the desire to adopt can cause people to financially lose their minds. I have coached families who bankrupted themselves with adoption fees and costs because their huge hearts blurred all logic and common sense. It will be difficult to raise money-smart kids who you adopted while you were money-crazy. Adoption can be done without debt if you follow some simple guidelines. Plan, plan, plan, and save, save, save. Once you have done that, then really study adoption and look closely into at least five to ten agencies. Truthfully, a lot of adoptions cost twice what they should. You really need to know for yourself what you are getting into so you don't pay way too much.

If you are planning to go this route, I recommend Julie Gumm's great book, *Adopt Without Debt*. Adopting is so emotional that you want to be very careful not to lose your mind and your money while trying to grow your family.

Raising Special Needs Children

Raising and caring for a special needs child is a wonderful but exhausting experience. Parents often ask how to teach a special needs child to be a money-smart kid and how to ensure her care. Obviously the level at which your child is functioning will dictate how and to what extent you can teach these principles. But I really encourage you to meet your child where she is and include money-smart teaching in everything you do. We have a good friend whose twenty-year-old has Down syndrome. He is fairly high-functioning, and his parents have taught him money skills his whole life. This has boosted his confidence, and his wonderful smile is often seen around a money transaction.

The only extra care you'll need in your estate plan is a Special Needs Trust. This trust is similar to leaving money in a trust at your death to care for your other minor children. The only difference is this trust will last for the child's entire life. You simply make this trust a part of your will and leave enough term life insurance to the trust so the child can live off the trust income the rest of his or her life. Once you have personally built wealth and are debt-free, you can let the insurance drop and leave enough of your wealth to the trust to create an income for this child.

What about Grandparents?

Hopefully your money-smart kid has money-smart grandparents. However, you should remember that even normally smart and well-balanced people have the potential to lose their minds at the sight of a grandbaby. If the grandparents are undermining your money-smart kid lessons and principles, take them to lunch or coffee and ask for their help. They really do love their grandchildren, and they really aren't trying to undermine your authority. They just see spoiling your child as their God-given right. It is a time-honored tradition for grandparents to allow their grandchildren to do things and eat things they never would have let their own children do. However, if this is an over-the-top pattern, not just an occasional blip, then a loving, smiling, firm discussion is necessary. A grandparent can be a great advocate in growing great kids when the grandparent is made a partner and not viewed as a problem. However, if, after some firm discussions, a grandparent continues to cross your financial boundaries, you may have to limit the grandparent's access to your child until the lesson is learned.

Now, what if you are a grandparent who has had to completely take over the parenting role? This is becoming more and more common in our culture. If you are a grandparent raising your grandchild, then you are simply taking on the role of parent. All the money-smart kid principles in this book apply.

THE GIFT OF DIGNITY

Rachel: I told you at the start of this chapter that it would cover a wide variety of family situations. In everything we've examined here, I hope you've noticed one key theme that runs through all the relationships in your child's life. That theme is the importance of boundaries. One of the most significant things my parents ever did for me was to simply *be my parents*. That meant they weren't my friends. They weren't my employees. They weren't my dictators. They were my *parents*.

No, they were not perfect. They made mistakes and messed up plenty of times. But they were intentional with putting boundaries in place, and they enforced consequences when those boundaries weren't respected. They were generous with their money, but they never allowed me to feel any ownership over it. They helped me when and how they could, but they weren't compelled to rescue me every time I messed up. They gave me an amazing life, but they made sure everything they provided would be a blessing, not a curse. As a result, they gave me an incredible gift. They gave me the dignity of becoming a responsible, self-supporting adult. Whether I'm working alongside my dad or doing something on my own, I know that I have what it takes to win. That's not coming from a place of arrogance; it's coming from a place of confidence. And that wealth of confidence is there because my parents put it there, slowly investing in me every time they enforced boundaries and made me struggle through something on my own. And I accepted those lessons as I got older and my maturity grew. Again, I don't want you to go crazy with this; like I said, I want you to bless your children as much as possible and to be reasonable! But with each of these opportunities, you should ask yourself, *Is this helping my child become the self-supporting, healthy, mature adult I want him to be?* That's a powerful question, and it may change a lot of your daily decisions as you encourage your children to be money-smart kids.

CHAPTER ELEVEN

Generational Handoff

Blessings or Curses

Rachel: I've noticed two distinct extremes when it comes to parenting. First, there are the straight-laced, locked-down, rule-setting, control-freak parents who try to force their kids into a tight little box where they have no opportunities to make any decisions on their own. Some of these kids grow up, run off to college, and drown in a puddle of beer. That's because they've never been given an ounce of freedom, so the first time they're away from Mom and Dad, they go completely crazy. They simply don't know how to make *good* decisions because they never had the chance to make *any* decisions.

Then there are the parents who seem to drift through life with no clear plan or boundaries—no rules, no guidelines. Discipline? That's a thing of the past. It's as though the parents are saying, "Fly, little eight-year-old, fly! Go freely. I'm sure you'll be just fine." Those are the kids you see at restaurants screaming and throwing silverware across the table while the parents sit there, seemingly clueless, as they enjoy what they think is a nice, quiet dinner. Those kids can't make good decisions because they've never been made to behave. Lucky for the next generation, these are not the only two options. There is a fantastic middle ground where your kids will be ready to accept the responsibility of adulthood someday.

LIVING BY THE ROPE

By now, I hope you've seen that my parents always tried to keep a balance between enforcing strict rule-following and allowing personal responsibility. They worked hard to give us the freedom to make our own decisions while still keeping us within the boundaries they set for us. They didn't do it perfectly every time, but I know the guidance they provided has been invaluable to my siblings and me.

Managing the Slack

One way Mom and Dad continually maintained a balance between grace and legalism was through the analogy of the rope. The Ramsey kids heard about the rope all the time. Our parents described it this way: "Picture an imaginary rope tied around your waist. I am holding the other end of the rope. The length of the rope is entirely up to me. A longer rope means you have more freedom to explore and make decisions, and a shorter rope means I have to rein you in a bit due to trust or behavioral issues."

For example, think about dropping your twelve-year-old daughter off at the movie theater. You tell her to stay inside the theater and that you'll be back in two hours to pick her up at that exact spot. When you come back to pick her up two hours later, she is nowhere to be found. You call her and find out she's across the street at the ice cream shop because she and her friends decided not to see a movie. So what happens? She loses some rope. You have to pull her back in a bit because she made a bad choice and didn't call to ask permission. Now, imagine your teenager is at a high school party where adult beverages are flowing. If he calls you, tells you what's going on, and asks you to come pick him up, then guess what? He just earned more rope because he showed the ability to make good decisions.

Kids want to be treated like adults. I used to say that to my parents all the time, and Dad always answered, "If you want to be treated like an adult, then act like an adult. Show me I can trust you, and I will." And Mom and Dad always followed through with that, giving me more freedom when I showed them I was worthy of their trust. Sure, there were times when they had to pull the rope back in because I made bad choices—there will always be a little back and forth—but you want the goal to be a nice, long rope by the time your kids leave home.

Letting Go

My sister, Denise, was the first Ramsey child to head off to college. Her last night in the house, Mom cooked a delicious family dinner and we all sat around the dining room table, laughing, crying, and telling stories about Denise. If you were just listening in, you would have thought we were at a funeral—but no, she was only moving a few hours away. As the night was winding down, Dad left the room and came back carrying a big gift bag. He sat down, reached in the bag, and pulled out a beautiful loop of thick, white rope. There were smaller ribbons woven into the rope, each one a different color.

He said, "Denise, your mom and I are so proud of you and the woman you've become. But starting tonight, things will be a little different." Then he explained what the different colored ribbons meant. There was a red ribbon signifying her academics, purple for her spiritual walk, white for her purity, green for her ability to handle money, orange for the University of Tennessee, and yellow as a reminder that she could always come home. When he was finished, Dad said, "Denise, we trust you. You make great decisions. You're going to be 250 miles away, and that means we can't hold the other end of the rope anymore." He paused, put the rope in Denise's hands, and said, "Honey, tonight we're giving you the rope." It was sweet and, sure, a little cheesy, but it was a powerful moment for all of us.

Several weeks later, on Parent Weekend at UT, we all visited Denise in her dorm room. Dad was shocked to see the rope hanging on her doorknob. When he asked about it, Denise said, "Oh, Dad, the rope is a legend. Girls come from all over the dorm to hear the story of the rope. They love it!"

As we were driving back to Nashville, Mom and Dad were talking about how shocked they were that the rope had made such a strong impact on Denise. I chimed in from the backseat and said, "It's not just Denise. That meant a lot to Daniel and me too."

Mastering the Rope

Growing up, I didn't really understand the significance every time Mom and Dad mentioned the rope. Looking back, however, I realize that my childhood was a twenty-year lesson in responsibility. They were preparing us all along to be wise, trustworthy adults. They knew we would be heading into an enormous responsibility some day. And no, I'm not talking about what they may or may not leave us when they're gone. I'm talking about the responsibility every child will face someday: adulthood. Every child will one day be an adult, making his or her own decisions and taking responsibility for his or her own life. Whether they win or lose, whether they're broke or wealthy, whether they're successful or miserable, it's up to them. As a parent, you're preparing your children to make the decisions that will determine the kind of life they'll have as adults.

One of the greatest gifts you'll ever give your child is preparing her to thrive as an adult. That happens through a lot of conversations, teachable moments, trial and error, and modeling wise behavior with money. And if you do the things we've been talking about throughout this book, your child *will* be wealthy one day. It's not a matter of income, remember? If your child grows up knowing how and why to work, spend, save, and give; if she knows how to budget; if she avoids debt of any kind throughout her lifetime; if she learns contentment from an early age; if she does all these things, and if you do all these things with your own money as well, then you should expect your child to become wealthy later in life. It's the natural byproduct of handling money God's ways.

So assuming your child will be responsible for managing a lot of money later in life, let's look at some key things you can do today to prepare her to truly manage that wealth with confidence and integrity. The first thing we need to deal with, though, is a massive cultural misunderstanding about money in general: the idea that building wealth is somehow immoral or wrong.

IS WEALTH EVIL?

Dave: There are numerous toxic money messages in our culture today that you must address yourself and insulate your children from. One pervasive message is that wealth is evil and wealthy people are all crooks who take advantage of others. This lie is causing an entire generation to wonder if they should go into the marketplace and attempt to win. Sadly, because winning usually has financial rewards, some people feel as if they have done something wrong when they win with money.

The Root of the Problem

The Bible does not say money is the root of all evil; it says the *love* of money is the root of all kinds of evil. Money is amoral; it does not have morals. Money is not good, and money is not bad. Money is like a brick: A brick can be used by good people to build hospitals, or it can be used by bad people to smash windows. The brick is not bad or good; the person holding it is.

The lie that says wealth and wealthy people are evil causes people to make bad decisions. If you believe the lie that money is evil and hurts people, why would you teach your children to win with money? And if you believe that lie, you certainly wouldn't leave your children money in your estate because you believe it would harm them. Even some wealthy people have believed this lie. They are afraid that if they leave wealth to their children, they will bring them great harm. That is sad because these parents miss the opportunity to train money-smart kids who could use the money to be world-changers.

The truth is, many wonderful families build wealth and leave it to money-smart kids, but you rarely hear about those families. They will never have their own reality show because it would be boring. Instead, we see trust-fund babies acting like idiots, and as we watch, we begin to fear that leaving our kids an estate will bring them great harm. Please understand, leaving adult children a great value system but little money is still a great legacy. But leaving adult children a great value system and wealth to impact and help others is a *stellar* legacy! Don't believe the toxic messages of our culture that say money is evil and wealthy people are all crooks. Those are gross generalizations. They are lies, and those lies could destroy your legacy.

SAFEGUARDING YOUR CHILDREN

Money is not evil, but it is very powerful, and, when handled by someone with a weak value system, it can be dangerous. There are some specific ways to safeguard your children against being harmed by the power of money. Obviously you will teach, guide, and provide a living example of the principles we have been exploring in this book. Doing that over twenty years usually creates an adult who can handle the weight of wealth.

The Ownership Principle

Teaching our children the principle of ownership is one of the strongest safeguards against money harming or destroying them. We must continuously remind our children that we don't own anything; we are just managers. We have mentioned this concept throughout this book, but consider carefully how this simple idea safeguards your child's heart. Owners have rights; managers have responsibilities. Owners think of themselves; managers can't. It isn't their money, so they must think of others. Owners worry over their money; managers don't need to worry because the money isn't theirs to begin with. Owners hold with a tight fist; managers hold with an open hand.

We start by teaching a small child to share, and we increase the sophistication of the discussion as they mature. If you can instill in your child's heart the idea that he is a manager, not an owner, you have given him a tremendous gift. You have safeguarded him from letting wealth ruin his life.

The Magnification Principle

Another safeguard you should instill in your children is the principle of magnification. Money magnifies whatever and whoever it touches. Wealth exposes people for who they really are—whether good or bad. If you have a temper, wealth will make you a raging lunatic. If you are a giver, wealth will make you a philanthropist. It is vital that you teach your children that their good and bad character traits will be magnified as they grow their wealth. Once children understand this idea, it gives pause to consider how they act and who they are striving to become.

The Community Principle

A third safeguard you can employ to keep the power of money from hurting your children is the community principle. Surrounding your children with adults and other children who have healthy value systems safeguards their hearts. It is also great to spend time with other families who are not only winning with money but also share your value system. It's good for your child to be friends with the son of a generous, wealthy man or for your daughter's best friend to have a mom who is a successful entrepreneur. These adults and children become the community that further insulates and safeguards your child's heart against wealth's potentially harmful effects and sets up positive opportunities for wealth to be a blessing instead. You should teach your children to be kind and willing to interact with virtually anyone from any background, but the point here is to be very intentional about who is influencing your child. They become who they hang out with.

DOING THE DETAILS

In our *Financial Peace University* class that's taught in churches and communities all over the country, families come together once a week for nine weeks to hear Rachel and me (plus other great speakers) teach them how money really works. We have lessons on saving, debt, smart shopping, giving, and all sorts of money-smart principles. But of all the topics we cover, the most important one is the budget lesson. No, learning how to do a budget isn't much fun, and it certainly isn't glamorous, but we've found the budget is the single most-important factor among people who win with money. Why? It's because details matter. You will never win with money by accident. In the same way, you're not going to pass on a financial legacy to your kids by accident. It takes planning, and it takes some time doing the details to get your children—and your estate—ready for the handoff.

Having "The Talk"

Throughout this book, we have taught you to make money-smart kid principles an ongoing, constant discussion with your children. As parents, you must strike a balance here. Don't obsess about money with them. At the same time, don't think your job is done because

235

you've had one "money talk" with them. *One* money talk won't cut it. Instead, make the discussion continuous like you do with other things you want to become part of your children's character. Some parents are so secretive and paranoid about money that they simply don't discuss it. As a result, their kids grow up in homes where the parents never talk about money and never talk about sex, so the kids assume the parents have neither! They are later shocked to find out their parents had both. This lack of communication leaves children completely unprepared to deal with these issues.

Family Constitution

I have found that many wealthy families have family constitutions stating what their families are all about—essentially their mission statements. This does not have to be a difficult or particularly detailed document. Ours isn't. As you can imagine, ours includes working, giving, investing, and avoiding debt. Our opening line is from the Bible: "As for me and my house, we will serve the LORD" (Joshua 24:15 NKJV). If you are not a person of faith, you would start yours differently, but you can still state what your family values are. The Ramsey family crest from our Scottish heritage uses the Latin phrase *Ora et Labora*: Pray and Work. High-quality organizations have clear vision and clearly stated values. This is also true of high-quality families. Take the time to write a family constitution. Read it to your kids, and refer to it often. They may not understand its impact at first, but over time it will show them that your family is committed to each other and has a purpose and a mission.

Estate Planning

This is not an estate-planning book—not even close. But my friends who are estate planners tell me that about 70 percent of Americans die without a will. That is ridiculous, not to mention really bad stewardship. When you die without having a current will and estate plan, you leave a huge mess for your family. The mess is legal, financial, relational, and emotional. A wonderful way to say "I love you" to your family is to have your estate plan completed in detail. One of the last teachable moments you will provide your money-smart kids (once they are adults) is to show them how to plan their estates and hand down wealth generationally.

When your will and estate plan is complete, you should have an informal reading of the will for all the adults involved, including your grown children, so everyone is clear about how you plan to handle your estate. You should walk through how the estate will be divided and what your intentions are. You can work out any potential problems or hurt feelings right then. This is to avoid the overly dramatic scene you've seen in too many movies where the trophy wife, the good child, and the evil stepbrother erupt into insanity after listening to the reading of the will. But that is not how life really works. Talk through your estate plan while you are alive so there won't be a major inheritance battle later.

Also, it's important to remember that fair does not mean equal. If one of my grown children is doing drugs and living a horrible life, he or she will get zero from my estate. This is not an act of punishment but an act of love. What loving parent would finance his child's drug problem? If you have a special needs child, he will likely need and get more so he is cared for adequately. If there are grown children from a first marriage and one of the parents remarried later, the grown children might get less than minor children who still need care. If you discuss your intentions with everyone involved and explain your reasoning in advance, you are doing your loved ones a great service. Way too many families waste time fighting over botched or neglected estate preparations while they are trying to grieve the loss of a loved one.

Get Organized

In our *Legacy Journey* class, members are given a wooden box that holds files and fits into a file drawer. We call it the Legacy Box. This box, or just your file drawer, should be the go-to place for all the paperwork that will be needed upon your death. Your spouse or children should be able to simply open that drawer and find the insurance paperwork, you and your spouse's wills, titles, investment statements, financial statement, and all other important papers necessary to manage your estate after your departure. There should be no mystery, no hidden documents, and no need for a metal detector in the backyard looking for buried jars of money. Completing your estate plan—including compiling a Legacy Box with all your important documents—and discussing your intentions while you are alive are two of the most loving acts you can do for your family and your grown money-smart kids.

Honoring Broke Parents

Grown children often ask me what their responsibility is to parents who are broke. A lady named Renée recently called my radio show, torn about what to do with her mom. Her mom was fifty-eight years old and had mismanaged money and overspent her entire life. She couldn't hold down a job because she didn't want to work, and when she did work, she went in late and was hard to get along with. Renée's mom was also a travel agent for guilt trips, telling her daughter that it is her biblical duty to support her. She often quoted "Honor your father and mother" to her.

The biblical mandate to honor your father and mother does not mean to finance their bad behaviors. If your dad is using cocaine, how does giving him money honor him? You can honor the person and the role of parent without being required to finance bad behavior. I certainly don't mind if you help with some basics, but even then, you need to be very careful to avoid enabling. You have to define what is really helping them and what is throwing money at them to get them to shut up.

On the other hand, there is the mom who has been faithful. She has been a good person, but she simply never made or saved much money. Obviously, this is a much more attractive person than Renée's mother, and it makes the decision to help much easier. Your first obligation is always to your own household and children, but helping parents when they truly need assistance is a fulfilling thing. A friend of mine has a wonderful father. This is a good man who has worked hard and has saved money, but he never made much, so he still had a mortgage going into retirement. It was a lot of fun to watch my friend pay off his dad's house. I'm pretty sure neither this father nor his son thinks wealth is evil.

The Greatest Investment

Managing wealth and passing it down generationally takes hard work and discipline. It also takes time—time to teach your kids the money-smart principles in this book. It doesn't happen overnight. Early on, you may have as many mess-ups as you have wins. That's okay. Keep at it. Put in the time, and use every opportunity you can to create teachable moments. If you do, eventually you'll see the fruit of your hard work. You'll get to watch as your grown kids go out on their own—confident, money-smart, and ready to take on the world. And you will know all that hard work was one of the greatest investments you ever made.

EMBRACING THE RESPONSIBILITY

Rachel: "Mom, are we rich?"

I was a little girl when I asked that question. Mom and Dad's bankruptcy was a decade or so behind them, and they had done an incredible job moving past it and building a new business. Dad's radio show was taking off, and his *Financial Peace University* class was growing nationwide. He had two *New York Times* best sellers by then, but his best-known book, *The Total Money Makeover*, was still just an idea knocking around in his head. It was definitely a time of transition for our family, and as I watched the financial stress of the last several years drain out of my parents, I had a sense that our money situation was changing.

Growing up, the Ramsey kids never had any idea how much money our parents made. I've told you what life was like for us when I was young. I was raised on second-hand, consignment-store clothes. Mom was the coupon queen. Dad was a master at flea-market bargaining. Our favorite restaurant was Sharon's Kitchen. Mom and Dad both drove cars with squealing brakes and torn interiors. Dad worked all day every day and several nights a week. Then, gradually, things began to change. You wouldn't notice it if you weren't really paying attention because the changes were so subtle. Dad was home more at night. The cars got nicer. We ventured outside our own kitchen for dinner occasionally. Our vacations had more sights to see than just our old tent and campgrounds. There was never a time when I thought, *That's it! We've finally made it. We're not broke anymore!* Like I said, it was a slow shift in what we were able to do. Our conversations about money didn't change, and how we handled money didn't change, but what we were able to *do* with our money did.

Flash forward another decade later. I was twenty-one, and I'd only been married a few months. College graduation was a month or so away, and I had already decided to move back to Nashville and join Dad in his crusade—*our* crusade—to spread the message of financial peace around the world. My husband and I walked into my parents' house and joined my brother and sister in the living room. Family meetings were not uncommon growing up in the Ramsey house, but when Dad called this particular meeting, we all had a feeling it was going to be a little different. We knew Mom and Dad had been doing some planning for the future because we'd already had a few conversations about their wills and estate plan. But tonight was different. Tonight, I was going to learn *everything*.

Dad walked us into the kitchen, and we noticed neatly prepared, meticulously organized folders at each seat around the table. I'll admit I was a little nervous. The first thing Dad said was, "Do not look ahead in your folder. This conversation will be a progression, and I don't want you to jump to the end." Then Dad talked about how much God had blessed our family, and he reminded us how difficult those early years had been for us. He talked about the sacrifices he and Mom had made and how committed they had been to handling money God's ways. He told us that money didn't have morals of its own; instead, it takes on the characteristics of the person holding it. He stressed how money magnifies everything, so it can make a generous person incredibly generous and a selfish person unbelievably selfish. He said money can be a blessing or a curse, and it all depends on our attitude and behaviors with money. He spoke of all the good we could do with money—for both our own family and the whole world—if we saw it as a tool to be used for the good of others. Finally, he said, "God's ways of handling money work. They worked for our family. But whatever you see in your folder isn't ours; it's God's. He's the owner, and we're the managers. We've been having these conversations with you kids your whole lives. Your mom and I know you can handle the responsibility we'll leave you one day. So it's time to take a look at what you'll be responsible for."

With that, we started looking through our folders. It was a full estate plan, showing every detail. For the first time in my life, I knew everything. As we were going through the folder, I was surprised by the fact that every single page, every number in every column, felt like a *responsibility*, not a sum of money. That weighed on me. I didn't want this responsibility to come between me and my husband or my siblings. I didn't want to mess up what Mom and Dad had done such a great job of building over the past two and a half decades. Sure, it was amazing to see a record of God's faithfulness and blessings, but the atmosphere around the kitchen table that night was serious. We weren't laughing and playing. This was a circle of adults who, together, were responsible for managing a portion of God's resources. The thing is, though, I wasn't scared. My parents had been preparing me for this my whole life. I knew how to handle money. I knew how to work, spend, save, and give. I don't know if you could say I was *born* for this, but I know without a doubt that I was *raised* for this. As we sat there going through everything that night, I thought back to that question I had asked my mom so many years before: "Mom, are we rich?"

"Yes, Rachel," she had replied. "We're rich in love."

Choose Life

"Rich in love"—that phrase has been ringing in my ears most of my life. When I was born in the middle of my parents' financial crash, I'm sure they didn't feel "rich." When Mom used coupons for every purchase and bought all our clothes at consignment shops, and when Dad had to work fifteen hours a day to put food on the table and pay off all their creditors, they didn't feel "rich." Even years later, as they built wealth and were able to afford nice things, they avoided the trap of feeling "rich" with money. Instead, they always kept their focus where it mattered: They determined that, no matter what, our family would be rich in love.

That was their decision, their commitment to handle money God's ways and to teach their children to do the same. It's the same decision you're facing right now. Deuteronomy 30:19 says, "I call heaven and earth as witnesses today against you, that I have set before you life and death, blessing and cursing; therefore choose life, that both you and your descendants may live" (NKJV). As we wrap up this book, I want you to think about all the ways we've discussed preparing your kids to win with money. You won't always get it right, but you have the power to pass on a legacy of blessing or cursing—life or death—to your children. If you're reading this book, it's clear which one you've chosen for your child. You chose life.

CHAPTER TWELVE

I Was That Dad . . .

Dave: I was that dad. At the beginning of this book, you read about the fabulous debt-free screams that occur in our lobby and are broadcast on *The Dave Ramsey Show*. Rachel described a typical family who visits our lobby, and she talked about how she saw herself in one of those little girls. She was that little girl whose parents had made mistakes but decided to make better decisions about their future, setting themselves free from debt. She was born the year we filed bankruptcy, so it is more than ironic that she has been called to teach this material.

I was that dad. I was the dad who made every financial mistake imaginable. Whatever you have done wrong, I have done it with zeros on the end. I was that dad who was broke and broken. I was that dad who did not have everything figured out. I was that dad who did not practice the money-smart principles in this book perfectly. Yet I was also that dad who won in spite of all my imperfections and mistakes.

Now you are that dad or mom. You don't have to be perfect in your handling or understanding of money to teach these concepts to your children. There are no perfect parents. We all know that, so give yourself some grace. But be in the game. Be in the fight to win your child's heart to money-smart principles. We were not perfect parents in the Ramsey house, but we kept at it. When we dropped a pass, we didn't quit the game and walk away. Instead, we threw the pass again and again, so that at least sometimes it was caught.

Teach It Like It Really Matters

There is a story in the Bible where Jesus teaches about the cost of discipleship. While walking along the road, He says to a man, "Follow Me." The man answers, "Lord, let me first go and bury my father." Jesus' response is kind of strange. He says, "Let the dead bury their own dead" (Luke 9:59–60 NKJV). The first time I read that verse, I thought Jesus actually told the man not to go to his own father's funeral! Then I heard Larry Burkett, a Christian financial teacher, offer a plausible explanation for Jesus' radical demand. Larry said that in Jewish tradition, on the day a man reached retirement age, he turned over all his wealth and possessions to the control of his oldest son. The oldest son then had the responsibility to take care of his parents, minor siblings, and unmarried sisters with that money. Larry suggested that the man's father had probably not yet died; he was simply ready to turn over his wealth to his son. So this son may have been saying to Jesus, "I will follow you, but first let me run home and pick up my dad's wealth."

A good friend of mine is a Jewish Rabbi, and he explained to me that, in the Jewish mind, money equals life. Therefore, no money equals death. I'm not saying that Jewish people are all about money. Instead, they realize that money gives them the ability to make a life. So for this son to "bury his father" meant his father was no longer in control of his money once he turned it over to his son.

Think about the implications of this cultural tradition. What if you knew from the time your oldest son was born that he would be tasked with taking care of you and your spouse in your golden years? What if the quality of your retirement years was based not on your 401(k) or your real estate holdings but instead on how competent your oldest son was with money? If you knew you were going to have to turn over your very existence and quality of life to that child someday, you would be very intentional about making sure that child knew how to handle money. You would teach him to work, give, save, and spend wisely. You would teach him about investments, taxes, and budgeting. You would teach him about contentment, debt, and generational estate planning. If you knew your quality of life and maybe even your very life depended upon your oldest son being competent with money, you would definitely make sure he was a money-smart kid. So why not be that intense and intentional about raising money-smart kids regardless of your faith or cultural traditions?

You Can Do This

I was that dad who made big money mistakes and failed. But I was also that dad who decided to change my family tree. I was that dad who realized that to *financially* change my family tree, I had to *intentionally* raise money-smart kids. Regardless of the stupid financial decisions you have made, you can turn your financial life around. Regardless of how late you begin teaching your kids to be money-smart, there is still hope. You get to decide that starting today, from this day forward, you are going to be intentional about not only your money but also in teaching the next generation.

Speaking as a very proud dad, I will tell you that the payoff is worth the trouble. Sharon and I feel great satisfaction and richness of soul as we stand back and watch how confident and competent our grown money-smart kids are. They are not perfect, but they are really doing well. They stand on their own and appear to have wisdom beyond their years. They are generous, frugal, and intentional in their money decisions. They don't have a dime of debt. But the most satisfying thing of all is that they are prepared and capable to take on the responsibility and legacy of managing wealth generationally. Rachel and I want that for you. So when your money-smart kids are grown, you can lean back in your chair with pride, knowing they are not only winning, but they are also capable of managing your legacy for generations to come.

This is *your* legacy. Now go make it happen.

Notes

Chapter 3

1. Karen J. Pine, "Report on a survey into female economic behaviour and the emotion regulatory role of spending," *Sheconomics*, 2009, accessed June 14, 2013, http://www.sheconomics.com/downloads/womens_emotions.pdf.

Chapter 4

1. "Majority of Americans Do Not Have Money Available to Meet an Unplanned Expense," *National Foundation for Credit Counseling*, accessed May 10, 2013, http://www.nfcc.org/newsroom/newsreleases/floi_july2011results_final.cfm.
2. Blake Ellis, "28% of Americans have no emergency savings," *CNN Money*, June 25, 2012, http://money.cnn.com/2012/06/25/pf/emergency-savings/index.htm.
3. Stephen Gandel, "Everything You Know About

Kids and Money Is Wrong," *CNN Money*, July 18, 2006, http://money.cnn.com/magazines/moneymag/moneymag_archive/2006/08/01/8382223/.

Chapter 5

1. W. Keith Campbell, Elise C. Freeman, and Jean M. Twenge, "Generational Differences in Young Adults' Life Goals, Concern for Others, and Civic Orientation, 1966-2009," American Psychological Association, 2012, http://www.apa.org/pubs/journals/releases/psp-102-5-1045.pdf.

Chapter 6

1. "2012 U.S. Banking Sector Outlook: Happy Days Are Gone Again," Trepp, December 22, 2011, http://www.trepp.com/2011/12/22/11707/.
2. Melanie Hicken, "Average wedding bill in 2012: $28,400," *CNN Money*, March 10, 2013, http://money.cnn.com/2013/03/10/pf/wedding-cost/.

Chapter 7

1. Blake Ellis, "Class of 2013 grads average $35,200 in total debt," *CNN Money*, May 17, 2013, http://money.cnn.com/2013/05/17/pf/college/student-debt/index.html.

Chapter 8

1. Blake Ellis, "Average student loan debt nears $27,000," *CNN Money*, October 18, 2012, http://money.cnn.com/2012/10/18/pf/college/student-loan-debt/index.html.
2. Rohit Chopra, "Student Debt Swells, Federal Loans Now Top a Trillion," Consumer Financial Protection Bureau,

July 17, 2013, http://www.consumerfinance.gov/speeches/
student-debt-swells-federal-loans-now-top-a-trillion/.

3. "Borrower in Distress: A Survey on the Impact of Private
Student Loan Debt," Young Invincibles, May 2013,
http://younginvincibles.org/wp-content/uploads/2013/05/
Borrower-in-Distress-5.8.13.pdf.

4. "Trends in College Pricing 2012," College Board Advocacy
& Policy Center, 2012, http://advocacy.collegeboard.org/
sites/default/files/college-pricing-2012-full-report_0.pdf.

5. Carol Hymowitz, "Any College Will Do," *The Wall Street
Journal*, September 18, 2006, http://online.wsj.com/article/
SB115853818747665842.html.

6. Zac Bissonnette, *Debt-Free U* (New York: Portfolio
Penguin, 2010), 217.

7. Blaire Briody, "When parents pay for college,
could kids' grades suffer?" *The Week*, January 23,
2013, http://theweek.com/article/index/239074/
when-parents-pay-for-college-could-kids-grades-suffer.

Chapter 9

1. Janine Eccleston, "Why The Halloween Industry Is Worth
$8 Billion," Investopedia, October 16, 2012, http://www.
investopedia.com/financial-edge/1012/why-the-halloween-
industry-is-worth-8b.aspx.

Chapter 10

1. "More Young Adults Are Living in Their Parents' Home,
Census Bureau Reports," United States Census Bureau,
November 3, 2011, http://www.census.gov/newsroom/
releases/archives/families_households/cb11-183.html.

Student Budget

Yes, this budget form has a lot of lines and blanks.
But that's okay. We do that so we can list practically every expense imaginable on this form to prevent you from forgetting something. Don't expect to put something on every line. Just use the ones that are relevant to your specific situation.

Step 1

Write your monthly income in the box at the top (**A**), including any money your parents give you. This is the amount you have to spend for the month. Pretty simple, right?

A ----------------------➤ INCOME

Step 2

At the bottom of the form, write your income in the Income box (**B**).

Step 3

Within each category, like Recreation, there are items like Movie and Sporting Event. Start at the top and work your way down, filling out the Budgeted column (**C**) first. Add up each subcategory and put that number in the Total box (**D**).

Step 4

Go through the form and add up all of the category Total boxes (**D**). Write that grand total in the Outgo box (**E**). That's how much you spend every month. The goal is to spend every dollar you make, but no more. So if your Outgo is greater than your Income, you need to bring down the budgeted amount on some items. If your Outgo is less than your Income, you need to increase the amount in some area like College savings or Restaurants.

Step 5

Once your Outgo is the same as your Income, write a zero in the Zero box at the bottom (**F**). You're done!

Student Budget

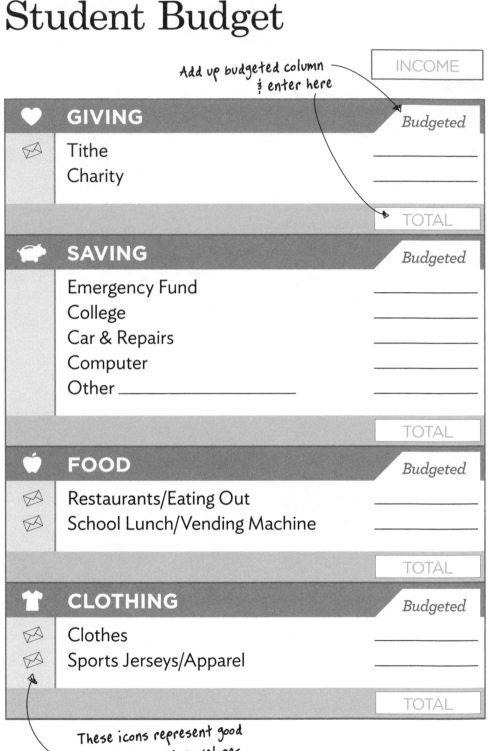

INCOME

Add up budgeted column & enter here

♥ GIVING

Budgeted

✉ Tithe _____

Charity _____

TOTAL

🐷 SAVING

Budgeted

Emergency Fund _____

College _____

Car & Repairs _____

Computer _____

Other _____ _____

TOTAL

🍎 FOOD

Budgeted

✉ Restaurants/Eating Out _____

✉ School Lunch/Vending Machine _____

TOTAL

👕 CLOTHING

Budgeted

✉ Clothes _____

✉ Sports Jerseys/Apparel _____

TOTAL

These icons represent good options for cash envelopes

🚗 TRANSPORTATION · *Budgeted*

Gas _____
Car Insurance _____
Oil Change _____
License & Taxes _____

TOTAL

🧍 PERSONAL · *Budgeted*

Cosmetics/Hair Care _____
Music/Technology _____
Gifts _____
Pocket Money _____
Cell Phone _____
Other _____ _____

TOTAL

🏃 RECREATION · *Budgeted*

Movie _____
Concert _____
Sporting Event _____
Other _____ _____

TOTAL

INCOME — OUTGO = ZERO

Add up totals from each category

Remember—The goal is to get this number to zero

Upcoming Expenses

How do you eat an elephant? One bite at a time.

You'll usually have a few big expenses, like a spring break trip, club dues, sports or music equipment and prom, throughout the year. These things can be budget busters if you don't plan ahead. Use this form to break down those upcoming expenses into bite-sized chunks for your monthly budget.

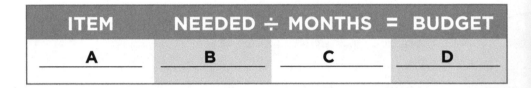

ITEM	NEEDED ÷ MONTHS = BUDGET		
A	B	C	D

Step 1

The Item column (**A**) lists common big expenses that you might need to plan for. If something is missing, fill it in as Other.

Step 2

For the items that apply to you, write how much money you'll need for that expense in the Needed column (**B**). Then figure out how many months you have to save up for that item, and write that in the Months column (**C**).

For example, let's say it's June and you want to spend $120 on Christmas presents for your friends this year. You'd need $120 by December, and you have six months to save.

Step 3

Now, for each item, divide the Needed amount by the Months you have. Write that in the Budget column (**D**).

So for Christmas, $120 divided by six months is $20 a month. That's how much you need to save each month to have $120 in time for Christmas. Now you can just put that $20 per month item on your monthly budget in the Savings category.

How much cash will you need?

How many months do you have?

Monthly amount for your student budget

ITEM	NEEDED ÷	MONTHS =	BUDGET
Homecoming	_____	_____	_____
School Club	_____	_____	_____
Sports Fees	_____	_____	_____
Christmas	_____	_____	_____
Valentine's Day	_____	_____	_____
Spring Break	_____	_____	_____
Anniversary	_____	_____	_____
Prom	_____	_____	_____
Other _____	_____	_____	_____
_____	_____	_____	_____
_____	_____	_____	_____
_____	_____	_____	_____
_____	_____	_____	_____
_____	_____	_____	_____
_____	_____	_____	_____
_____	_____	_____	_____

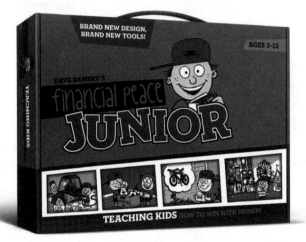